The Growth Spiral

Hans Christoph Binswanger

The Growth Spiral

Money, Energy, and Imagination in the Dynamics of the Market Process

Springer

Hans Christoph Binswanger
Institute for Economy and the Environment
University of St.Gallen
St. Gallen, Switzerland

Revised translation of the book "Die Wachstumsspirale", published with Metropolis-Verlag, 2006.

ISBN 978-3-642-31880-1 ISBN 978-3-642-31881-8 (eBook)
DOI 10.1007/978-3-642-31881-8
Springer Heidelberg New York Dordrecht London

Library of Congress Control Number: 2012950381

Printed on acid-free paper

Springer is part of Springer Science+Business Media (www.springer.com)

Preface to the German Edition

The concept of "economic growth" became a slogan during the 1960s. It replaced the idea of "reconstruction," which had guided economic activity since the end of the Second World War. The new slogan implied a return to the process of economic development of the nineteenth century which had been interrupted by two world wars and the Great Depression. However, before the 1960s "economic growth" had not been explicitly formulated as a concept, nor did the idea of the social product—today we talk of Gross Domestic Product (GDP)—represents statistically the annual product of goods. So far, it had never been imagined that GDP should continually increase from one year to the next by a constant percentage. This was quite new—even for an economist like myself who completed his studies at the end of the 1950s.

Until that time, the main object had been to find a way to prevent an interruption of the steady circulation of goods and money by the ups and downs of cyclical movements. But now it became a matter of extending the cyclical movements into a spiral, so that each cycle of economic activity would progressively augment production. At the time, I asked myself whether it was even possible for production to increase at a constant rate each and every year and hence exponentially. Was this not in contradiction with the first law of thermodynamics, according to which nothing in the physical world can increase, if not something else decreases? I looked for an answer in economic theory, which during the 1970s became increasingly concerned with the question of growth. But its findings left me unsatisfied, because increasing production was always attributed to "technical progress" in one form or another. But how could "technical progress" that comes from human knowledge result in quantitative economic growth? I could never get this question out of my mind, and it has remained there throughout all my years of research.

At the beginning of my academic career, I was preoccupied with policy-relevant questions. Over many years I studied issues related to European integration. I was particularly interested in studying the economic significance of a common currency as compared to multiple convertible currencies. This led me to pay greater attention to the interaction of real and monetary factors in the economic process, as shown in my book "Markt und international Währungsordnung" (*The Market and the International Monetary Order*).

In due course, my interests shifted to questions relating to the natural environment. This led me into an intensive study of the natural foundations of economic activity, since it was obvious that the production of waste and emissions which are harmful to the environment was closely related to the input of energy and raw materials taken from natural resources and used in the economic process. This work has found its way into two publications: "Wege aus der Wohlstandsfalle" (*Ways out of the Welfare Trap*) with W. Geissberger, T. Ginsburg, and others, and "Arbeit ohne Umweltzerstörung" *(Employment Without Environmental Destruction)* with H. Frisch, H. Nutzinger, B. Schefold, G. Scherhorn, U. E. Simonis, B. Strümpel, and V. Teichert.

While working on these books, it became clear to me that both the money and the natural world played a much greater role in the economy than conventional economic theory has assumed. And so I formulated a new approach to understanding growth which, in my opinion, cannot be explained without including the contribution of monetary dynamics and of the role of natural resources in the modern economy. This led me to reconsider the general foundations of economic theory from the perspective of economic growth including money and natural resources. The result is presented in this book. It aims to provide some guidance to all those who have to make decisions concerning, in one way or another, future economic development, and who therefore have to deal with the opportunities as well as the risks of economic growth.

This book addresses both the economic specialist and the interested lay reader. It makes reference to various specific schools of thought and economic thinkers. It does not, however, assume any prior knowledge of these, since the main lines of argument and their conclusions are established without any specific recourse to such references.

My work on this book would not have been possible without the assistance of many people. First of all I would like to express my thanks to Guido Beltrani, who played a major role for the completion of this book. His dissertation "Monetäre Aspekte des Wirtschaftswachstums" (*Monetary Aspects of Economic Growth*) took up the elements of my thinking on the growth imperative that had been contained in preliminary studies for this book. His own findings have, in turn, found their way into this book. This is especially true for the chapter on "The Avoidance of Losses as the Growth Imperative" in Part III. Consequently, he is named there as co-author.

I wish to thank Joseph A. Weismahr for important references and suggestions relating to the theory of production and distribution from the perspective of an entrepreneur, and my colleague Erwin Staehelin for expert assistance in the presentation of company balance sheets.

Further special thanks are due to my colleagues Hans Nutzinger and Johannes Schmidt for their critical reading of the text and for valuable suggestions.

Important for the completion of the work on this book was the fact that I was allowed to continue working at the Institute for Economy and Environment of the University of St. Gallen, where I had worked before my retirement. For this, and for the attention given to my work, I owe special thanks to the Directors of the Institute, my colleagues Thomas Dyllick and Ernst Mohr. I am also greatly indebted to the Institute's secretaries, Marlise Dreier and Vreny Knöpfler Mousa, for their untiring contributions in completing the manuscript and for never losing patience after many revisions. Christian Berger was of great practical help in designing the formal layout of the final version. I am very grateful to him for his work.

I am extremely grateful to my wife for the stamina she displayed in taking care of many things that I should have done, but did not do, while being busy with writing this book.

It was also a great pleasure that I was able to discuss this book with my sons, the economists Mathias and Johannes and the mathematician Klemens. Their knowledge of recent theoretical developments was a major contribution, and their open criticism has kept me from many errors. To them I dedicate this book.

St. Gallen (Switzerland), May 2006 Hans Christoph Binswanger

Preface to the English Edition

With modern economies becoming increasingly unstable, a critical evaluation of the conventional economic theory has become more and more crucial. Therefore, I decided to present an English version of my book "Die Wachstumsspirale," which had first appeared in German in 2006. This book offers a new theoretical approach to understanding the modern economy, focusing on its dynamic aspects. This approach stands in contrast to the static equilibrium concept which has been the foundation of conventional economics. The English translation presents these ideas to a wider audience aiming to promote the renewal of economic theory.

The English version largely corresponds to the German version. However, the text has been shortened in various sections in order to focus on the main thrust of the book.

Many people have contributed to the translation. A first translation was made by Keith Tribe, David Andersen, and the staff of "Profi-Fachübersetzungen." For further revisions of the translation I am grateful to Christian Berger, Hans Christoph Curtius, Philipp Friebe, Albert Gebhardt, Giulia Mennillo, and my sons Mathias, Klemens, and Johannes. For additional support, I am indebted to my colleagues Andreas Grüner, Fleming Ruud, and Erwin Staehelin and for many special advices to Josef A. Weissmahr.

I substantially benefitted from the opportunity to continue my work at the Institute for Economy and the Environment. In this respect I am obliged to my colleagues Thomas Dyllick and Rolf Wüstenhagen. Very special thanks go to Vreny Knöpfler-Mousa for the careful preparation of the manuscript and for always being ready to rewrite numerous versions of the manuscript.

The translation of the book was supported by the Bühler-Reindl-Fonds of the University of St. Gallen. This support is gratefully acknowledged.

St. Gallen(Switzerland), Spring 2006 Hans Christoph Binswanger

Contents

1 Introduction

Growth! Growth of gross domestic product! That is a goal on which the world's nations all agree. This imperative is taken for granted, and no further explanation is needed. Everything else seems to follow from its achievement.

In the past it was not always assumed that economies grew and should grow. The first signs of growth can be found in ancient times. But the European economy experienced sustained growth for the first time in the era of discovery and conquest. This led to an enormous influx of gold and silver from America, which financed the growth of sea trade and created a global trading network. The actual takeoff started, on one side, with the invention of paper money in the seventeenth century and, on the other side, with the invention of the steam engine in the eighteenth century. Paper money and the later creation of money by banks, together with the steam and the electronic technology, created the conditions for the industrial revolution of the nineteenth and the twentieth century.

Of course, crises during the nineteenth century were still frequent, mostly brought about because paper money had still to be backed by gold. It was only after the two world wars of the twentieth century that the link was broken completely, enabling a constant and sustained period of growth in the second half of the century.

But soon the "Limits to Growth" became an issue. This was the title of a report published by the Club of Rome in 1972, signed by Donella Meadows, Dennis L. Meadows, Jorgen Randers, and William W. Behrens. This report warned of the catastrophic consequences that would result from continuous growth in a finite world. Specific limits were identified: the exhaustion of natural resources, environmental crisis resulting from the buildup of waste and emissions, and the finite nature of food supply relative to the size of a growing population. Discussion of these limits led to the principle of sustainability established at the 1992 Rio de Janeiro conference, which set a global standard for economic development. The central idea was, along with the guarantee of free and fair development opportunities for the Third World, the principle of moderation in the use of natural resources. The exploitation of natural resources should be regulated in such a way that it enables future generations to enjoy the same opportunities as those enjoyed by the present generation.

H.C. Binswanger, *The Growth Spiral*, DOI 10.1007/978-3-642-31881-8_1,

However, the limits to growth turned out to be less severe than the report of the Club of Rome originally had anticipated. This made it possible to focus the concept of sustainability on a limited number of issues: above all, on the deterioration of the climate as a result of the increase in the emissions of greenhouse gases. Subsequently, there has been little talk of general limits to growth. The postulate of sustainability became an additional goal instead of replacing the goal of growth. In case of any conflict between the two goals, growth always has had priority.

The increasingly powerful quest for economic growth contrasted with the inability of the conventional economic theory to adequately capture the phenomenon of growth. The reason for this is the fact that the core of today's conventional theory is based on the neoclassical model of general equilibrium, as developed by Léon Walras (1834–1910).[1] He treats the market as a series of barters between individual economic entities, which are, in principle, self-sufficient and exchange only their surpluses. In this model, the marginal utility of goods and the marginal productivity of the production factors decrease, if more goods are produced. The variations in relative or so-called real prices in the barter process under perfect competition, determined by supply and demand, always result in an equilibrium. This presupposes that all relevant resources are scarce and appropriated and that variations in the prices of resources facilitate the optimal use. This is referred to as optimal allocation. Both equilibrium and optimal allocation are inherently static. If achieved, there are no gains nor losses from changing economic activity any further. Hence, there is also no incentive for growth.

In reality, the social product has always continued to increase. To explain this continuous growth, conventional economics had to refer to "exogenous factors," not included in the model itself. Initially, "technological progress" was used to square the circle between the growth of the social product and the static character of the model. "Technological progress" was introduced as a residual. It was simply assumed that this variable increased from year to year. Hence, economic growth was simply "explained" by introducing an assumption.

Since then, other factors have been proposed additional to "technological progress." The most important among them are "learning by doing," the increase in the stock of skills and knowledge through constant training and education, and the promotion of productivity by the formation of industrial "clusters," among others. These factors can reinforce each other: Experience accumulates, improved education and training today improves future education and training, and the "clusters" interact and grow stronger. This is called "endogenous growth." Of course, the inclusion of such factors made growth theory more substantial. But this "endogenization" remains

[1] The influence of Walras on conventional economic theory has been emphasized by Paul Samuelson, author of the most popular economics textbook (Samuelson and Nordhaus 1995). In his 1962 Presidential Address to the American Economic Association, he stated that "Most of the literary and mathematical economic theory appearing in our professional journals is more an offspring of Walras than anyone else" (Samuelson 1966, p. 1501). See also Wilfried Holleis (1985) for an account of the significance of Walras for conventional theory.

nevertheless incomplete, since the factors in question are also not integrated into the model of general equilibrium. With regard to the underlying model, they remain exogenous factors, just like "technological progress."

Under such circumstances, it is no wonder that, having largely attributed the process of growth to exogenous factors, responsibility for its maintenance was also transferred to an exogenous institution: the state. It is the state's task to provide more education and training, intensify competition, strengthen industrial clusters, and so on. But none of this is supported by any verifiable relationship between government activity and the market process. This is because the neoclassical theory has no room for the activity of the state.

Yet, economic growth, which represents an intrinsic part of the modern economy, cannot be explained by various constructs that are merely assumed and, as such, are nothing but stopgaps. Therefore, the underlying theory itself must be modernized. The factors and conditions characterizing the modern economy have to be integrated into the theory so that the growth tendency of the modern economy can be properly explained. This is not possible without taking account of the temporal dimension of the economic process—since growth takes time!—and so getting rid of the idea of a static equilibrium.[2]

The present investigation of the "growth spiral" is an attempt to build the foundations for a new theory of the modern economy. It is based upon the following premises, each of which takes account of time in a particular way:

> The market is fundamentally different from barter between individual economic agents which are in principle self-sufficient. It is based on the interaction of firms (which specialize in production) and households (which specialize in consumption). Production in firms opened the way for the gradual development for the comprehensive division of labor that cannot develop in a barter economy.
>
> Firms are artificial constructs that need capital in the form of money advances, with which they can purchase productive services from households *before* earning money from the sale of the products. To offset the risk associated with these advances, the firm expects a profit that equals or, if possible, exceeds the compensation of this risk.
>
> Money is an integral part of the modern economy. The influence of money has been further increased by the creation of money in the banking system. Banks can advance credits to firms on the basis of money creation. The firms use them for investment and hence for the increase in production. Therefore, the increase of the quantity of money has a direct influence on the growth of the real social product.
>
> Besides labor, today the most important factor of production is energy, which is constantly extracted from natural recourses.
>
> Human imagination constantly invents or discovers new products which meet new wants. Therefore, imagination has become an important factor of production in itself, complementing labor and energy.

[2] See Elisabeth Allgoewer (1992) for a discussion of the necessity—and difficulty—of including time in economic theory.

> The use of nature as a resource or a location for economic production, as well as a reservoir for waste and emissions, crowds out in many respects nature as living space. As a consequence, nature becomes more and more scarce. But since living space is not appropriated as such, and since consequently there is no price for it, this scarcity is not reflected in higher prices. Hence, economic growth continues without being impeded by the increasing scarcity of living space.

These principles broadly supersede the internal limits to growth implied by the modeling assumptions of neoclassical theory—the falling demand for goods due to their diminishing marginal utility and the decreasing marginal productivity of the production factors.

It follows from these principles that competition in the modern economy does not lead to a general equilibrium and an optimal allocation of scarce resources. Rather, competition brings about a constant tendency to transformation and growth. The economic process cannot be conceived as a circular flow in which the income that households receive from firms is equal to their expenses on goods purchased from firms. Household income instead grows with every circular flow because of the investment financed by newly created money together with an increasing stream of natural resources, including energy. In this way the circular flows, which formerly had prevailed, turned out into an *upward-moving spiral*. In each round the growth process creates more possibilities for growth, which in turn induces further growth. By contrast, where growth is insufficient, profits diminish, leading to a reverse spiral, which ends in losses and in a shrinking process. This results in a growth *imperative*.

Conventional economic reasoning still remains fully committed to neoclassical theory and has consequently become stuck in a dead-end street. There is only one way out of this dead end: Retreat back (at least) to the place where one has been *before* entering the dead-end street. In our case, this place is the classical theory.

The classical theory was primarily established by Adam Smith (1723–1790). A return to his ideas makes it possible to understand the market process in its temporal dimensions. But this does not mean that we should only go back to the classical theory. We need to go back also to the preclassical schools of thoughts, to the Mercantilists who emphasized the role of money, and to the Physiocrats who put more emphasis on the role played by nature. Nevertheless, we also need to move forward so that we can take into account the greater complexity of the modern economy. On the one hand, this means incorporating those elements of neoclassical theory that remain useful and valid—this involves mainly the derivation of demand from marginal utility—and, on the other hand, the findings of the historical school that developed in the nineteenth century and put the whole economy in a temporal context.

Important progress in economic thought was brought about by John Maynard Keynes (1884–1946), who showed that money does play a decisive role in the economic process. He overturned the neoclassical theory according to which money has no effect on real economic activity. However, his impact on economic theory faded in the last decade of the twentieth century, because his theorizing was too much focused on business cycles. As economic growth became the center of public attention instead of business cycles, interest in his work diminished. It is our task now to go back to Keynes' insights about the decisive role of money for economy activity. But now, we have to concentrate on the role of money for economic growth.

Our new approach allows us to overcome the distinction between micro- and macroeconomics and the division between general economics and the science of business administration. In this approach, the various special theories can be understood simply as a more thorough explanation of a coherent economic theory.

This book is divided into three parts.

Part One deals with the market as the interaction between firms and households, including the analysis of money and money capital. Firms are artificially constituted agents built on money capital and therefore (mainly) profit oriented, whereas household are natural, living agents, and therefore (mainly) utility oriented.

Our description of the market process is based upon the classical time-oriented model of demand and supply, which is much more realistic than the conventional neoclassical conception of static equilibrium prices. The classical theory can take account of gains and losses of the firms and so provide an explanation for the dynamics of the market.

By integrating money into the market mechanism, it is possible to overcome the dichotomy of prices and values and so the distinction between the explanation of relative or real prices and the explanation of the general price level. A special theory of money is no longer needed.

Part Two deals with the process of production and distribution, including energy and natural resources as well as human imagination. By recognizing that the natural and imaginary inputs into economic activities can be constantly extended, the neoclassical theory based on the idea of decreasing marginal productivity is replaced by the theory of net product. This theory is built upon the distinction between restitution costs, which have always to be covered so that production can continue, and the net product or surplus that allows higher consumption and promotes further development and growth. The theory of net product is based on an extension of the mercantilist, physiocratic, and classical approaches.

Upon these foundations, Part Three presents the growth spiral and its intrinsic drive for growth. Microeconomics and macroeconomics become unified, as microeconomic behavioral parameters are built into macroeconomic equations. The growth imperative is manifested in a critical minimal rate of growth, which allows firms to make always profits in the aggregate. If the growth rate falls below the critical growth rate, this will no longer be possible and the economy starts to shrink.

The Conclusion and Outlook chapter briefly deals once again with the dynamics of growth and makes clear the need to be aware of the inherent instability of growth as well as of the fundamental impossibility of infinite growth in a finite world.

Part I

Money and the Market

2 The Difference Between Market and Barter: Money and the Making of Markets

Market is in many respects distinct from barter. This distinction needs to be emphasized, because the conventional theory treats market and barter erroneously as the same.

Barter is essentially bilateral in nature. It requires the reciprocity of supply and demand. The supplier has to demand the good that the demander of his goods offers and vice versa. Further, when both—the supplier and the demander—have found an exchange partner, they still have to agree on the relative price which both can accept. This is a disadvantage, because for every new exchange a new price has to be found. Competition, and hence the efficiency of economic activity, is therefore restricted in two ways. First of all, there is the difficulty in finding a suitable exchange partner. Secondly, since the prices are necessarily expressed in different (real) units, parties cannot compare systematically across a range of supply and demand the prices and in this way look for the cheapest supplier or the best bidder.

On the other hand, barter has the advantage that, if an exchange takes place, demand and supply are always in equilibrium, and consequently the earnings and the expenditures of the exchanging parties are equal. This follows from their agreement on the relative price, without which there would be no exchange. *If* there is an exchange at an agreed price, then the value of whatever is supplied matches the value of what is demanded. For example, if apples and pears are exchanged and the agreed relative price is 2 kg of apples are worth 1 kg of pears, one of the parties gives up at this relative price 100 kg of pears and receives from the other party 200 kg of apples. For him therefore

$$100\,\text{kg pears} \times \frac{2\,\text{kg apples}}{1\,\text{kg pears}} = 200\,\text{kg apples}.$$

The other exchanging party gives at this price 200 kg of apples for 100 kg of pears. And so for him

$$200\,\text{kg apples} \times \frac{1\,\text{kg pears}}{2\,\text{kg apples}} = 100\,\text{kg pears}.$$

H.C. Binswanger, *The Growth Spiral*, DOI 10.1007/978-3-642-31881-8_2,

This means that at the relative price at which supply and demand are equal, earnings and expenses for both partners are also equal.

This is different in a market. Since the supply of a good is equal to the demand for money and the demand for a good is equal to the supply of money, the prices are money prices or absolute prices and therefore comparable. These money prices are the result of supply by many and demand by many. But, in contrast to barter, there is no necessity that earnings and expenses of individual market participants and supply and demand always match. Every individual, if he wishes to avoid being in debt, has only to make sure that he does not spend more money today than was earned before and has now in his hand. Whether this is the case is quite independent of whether there happens to be an equality of supply and demand in the market. By contrast with barter, trading in the market—buying and selling—occurs independently of the solvency or insolvency of individual participants or whether prices have managed to match supply to demand. Equilibrium is not a precondition for trade!

If we therefore compare market and barter, we can first of all say that the market is efficient, while barter is not. Secondly, while barter is necessarily always in equilibrium, the market is not.

Léon Walras, the founder of the neoclassical theory on which the conventional theory still rests, refused to recognize this conclusion. This was because he wanted to prove that the market process, if allowed to develop unimpeded, was capable not only to efficiently coordinate the plans of individual agents through the price mechanism but would also lead to a *general* equilibrium in which at each moment the expenditures of all parties were matched by their earnings. This would mean that they only spent what they simultaneously earned. To persuade those who doubted this, he was convinced that economics had to be put on a mathematical basis.[1] This can be presented in a much more elegant fashion if based upon a model of barter in which all actions occur simultaneously, rather than upon a market model in which time-dependent disequilibria have to be taken into account.

To this end Walras constructed a mathematical model for a quasi-market process which combined the advantages of barter—the constant realization of general equilibrium—with those of markets—the realization of efficient competition based upon a single market price for each good.

This model rests on the multilateralization of barter, such that instead of two exchanging parties with two goods, there are n exchanging parties with m goods. The exchanging parties are, as in bilateral exchange, independent "households," that is, economic agents which are engaged in production and consumption and are primarily self-sufficient, which only exchange what they do not themselves consume. Such exchanging parties can be understood to use the image favored by neoclassical theory, as many Robinson Crusoes who, instead of living in an isolated

[1] See Günther Hesse (1986, p. 81). He summarizes a report in which Walras describes himself how he came to formulate his theory mathematically. Hesse referred to Walras (1936, p. 466). The relationship of Walras to mathematics is dealt with in greater detail by Andreas Jäger (1999).

island, work on farms, which border each other.[2] Hence, they are able to engage in a common "marketplace." The quantity of exchangeable goods is in Walras's view fixed and less than would be demanded if the price were zero. They are, as a consequence, always limited relative to wants, that is, they are scarce.

This model was extended by Walras to include the factors of production. Since their prices are derived from the price of the products, and the factors of production and the products are exchanged simultaneously, so their respective prices are simultaneously determined. This model implied that production required no time, that is, that time is of no consequence. In this case, the scarcity of the factors of production can simply replace the scarcity of goods. Therefore, the quantities of factors of production rather than the quantities of goods are treated as given. That the supply of production factors might be extended as a *result* of the market process is ruled out.

One can think of this quasi-market as organized in the following way, as Walras himself indicated. Once a week, say on Monday, there is a market (see Patinkin 1965, 4 ff.). All "market participants" meet up on a marketplace, in the middle of which there is an auctioneer. The auctioneer selects a standard good or *numéraire*. The prices of all goods are expressed as their exchange ratio with this good. If the *numéraire* is wheat, then the price of apples is the quantity of wheat that is received for 1 kg of apples. Prices are hence always relative prices expressed in relation to the standard good which itself exchanges one for one, and so its relative price is 1. Instead of a particular standard good, it is also possible to choose an "average good," or a basket of goods, in which there is one nth of a unit of all n goods. One unit of the basket of goods therefore exchanges likewise at 1:1.

The "market" process begins with the auctioneer arbitrarily naming a price (*crié au hasard*) for each good including the factors of production, which is the same for all "market" participants. The auctioneer asks then the participants to name the desired quantities of goods to be demanded or supplied at this price. He sums up all these quantities when he has had the relevant responses. The auctioneer will then presumably establish that at the arbitrary price for one good demand exceeds supply, while for another good the supply exceeds demand. Where the demand is too great or the supply too small, the auctioneer will in the second round raise the price, and where the demand is too small or the supply too great, the price will be reduced. This process will continue until for every good or production factor, there is an equilibrium of supply and demand. To equalize earnings and expenditure, each independent economic unit must make its own calculation that conforms to the "exchange equation," which requires that for all transactions of an independent economic unit completed on that Monday, there is an equality of earnings and expenditures. Only at these equilibrium prices are the goods and products exchanged. And so with the help of the auctioneer, a bilateral barter is transformed into a multilateral barter. It is of decisive importance that in this model, the main

[2] The metaphore of Robinson Crusoe was introduced by Eugen von Böhm-Bawerk (1889, p. 109).

feature of bilateral barter is maintained: All prices at which transactions are undertaken are equilibrium prices. No transactions take place outside equilibrium!

Equilibrium means:

Firstly, the supply of *each* good is equal to the demand (market equilibrium).

Secondly, the earnings for *every* economic unit equal its expenditures (exchange equilibrium).

Walras found it necessary to reduce a market economy to a barter economy since in the process of barter time stands still for as long as negotiation takes place. There is therefore no need to take account of disequilibria which might put into question the consistency of the system. During the process of negotiation, all prices and quantities are only calculated entities and so open to revision. During this suspended "time," the economic units calculate the optimal use of goods on the basis of their preferences, taking account of the "exchange equation." Given the role of the auctioneer, perfect information prevails. At every moment every partner knows what will be received in return for a good. Therefore, it does not matter whether one negotiates on the basis of prices or of quantities. The result is the same.

Exchange is only completed if the parties to it agree on the equivalent values of exchanged goods, in other words, on the (relative) prices. Once this has happened, there is no further reason for the revision of the plans for supply or demand, but only a reason for their repetition. New adjustments are made only because of exogenous changes.

The Walrasian model of general equilibrium that represents multilateral barter is constructed as an analogue of the situation of bilateral barter, namely:

- The "conversation" between the auctioneer and the exchange partners constitutes the phase of negotiation that precedes each barter and during which time is "frozen."
- General equilibrium describes the situation after the end of negotiations, when the goods are handed over.
- The number and quantity of exchangeable goods or production factors is given a priori; they are simply a "legacy" of the past and have not to be further analyzed.

In this model, money functions only as a means of calculation and at the most additionally as a store of value.

A model of this kind can be formulated as a system of simultaneous equations in which all relative prices and quantities supplied and demanded are simultaneously explained.

Walras set economics off down the wrong track with his idea of general equilibrium, not because he set up a "pure theory" or a simplified model—such simplification is perfectly admissible in seeking to explain how barter works—but because the market economy is a money economy, not a barter economy. The creation of a "market" around an auctioneer, involving millions of "market" partners and millions of goods, is conceivable, but not feasible. That much is immediately apparent. The transition from bilateral barter to the multilateral market occurred not through the extension of barter to ever more partners and goods, but instead through the *substitution* of barter by payment with money.

The substitution of barter by money makes possible the emergence of efficient markets for each good or production factor tending to a single unique market price for each good or production factor. No longer is it necessary for earnings and expenditures of each individual economic unit to be at all times in equilibrium. Of course, in this case, the market cannot eo ipso guarantee on optimal coordination of individual plans under *given* conditions. But it possesses instead a dynamism that tends to *alter* given conditions by extending the scope for economic activity. Insofar as money is a "temporary" good which possesses value by virtue of it being spent at a *later* point in time on a good that one would like to have, or which is invested so that at a *later* point in time one might receive more money, it gives time both for promoting either a convergence between supply and demand within a *given* framework *or* preventing such convergence by actively *altering* the given framework. This means that market and competition not only coordinate but also lead the economy into constant forward motion. Whether convergence or forceful stimulus dominates depends on the options available to the firms.[3]

[3] It should be noted here that a clear distinction has to be made between the dynamisation of economic theory through the inclusion of money and the "dynamization" of Walrasian equilibrium on the part of Arrow and Debreu (1954), Debreu (1959), and Arrow and Hahn (1971). Arrow and Debreu do start out from the principle that there is a market not only for present but also for future goods. To this extent they do include time. However, trading in the market for future goods occurs in just the same way that trading in the market for present goods. These markets "'telescope' the future into the present" (Arrow and Hahn 1971, p. 33). The prices of all present and future goods come together into equilibrium in the present simultaneously. This excludes any genuine dynamics resulting from the successive variation from period to period of the quantities of resources employed and the composition of goods, both of these variations being the outcome of the actions and reactions of competitors in a historical process. The "dynamic" of Arrow and Debreu is a pseudo-dynamic. It remains stuck in a static model. Mark Blaug commented on the formalism of Arrow and Debreu as follows: "The Arrow–Debreu paper was devoted to a rigorous proof of the existence of a competitive general equilibrium of prices and quantities for a world in which commodities are produced and sold in every possible period and in all possible circumstances. . . . It employed set-theoretical mathematical techniques and the then relatively new theory of games and was almost immediately hailed as the alpha and omega of mathematical economics. . . . It took years if not decades to recognize that such a proof for a hopelessly abstract economy, however accomplished as an exercise in mathematics, teaches almost nothing about the substantial operation of a market economy; it is empirically empty" (Blaug 1999, p. 271).

3 Capital and the Firm: The Firm as the Engine of the Market Process

3.1 Capital as a Promotion Factor

The essence of the market is the interaction between firms, which produce, and households, which buy the products of the firms and sell labor and other factors of production to the firms.

Firms are artificial units, which need money in advance for enabling them to purchase labor and other factors of production *before* they can start the production process. The money advanced equals the firm's capital. With the possession of capital, firms can concentrate the production on specific products, using the advantages of the division of labor. Therefore, we can consider capital as a promoter of the division of labor. In this sense, capital is not a production factor but a promotion factor, responsible for the immense increase of production and productivity induced by the division of labor.

Since capital is an advance, it bears the risk to which any advance is exposed.[1] Since the advance can only generate a return after it has been invested, it is lost if the products to be sold tomorrow cannot be sold at a price which at least covers its costs. Risk has to be matched by the expectation of entrepreneurial profit, when capital is to be invested. This profit will "repay" the work of promotion done by capital taking account of the risk involved.

This conception of capital as a promotion factor is a consequence of the classical theory of supply and demand, developed by Adam Smith in his book *An Inquiry into the Nature and Causes of the Wealth of Nations*, first published in 1776. He recognized that the firms, which assembled workers in factories or in large-scale agricultural enterprises, separated these workers from their original source of subsistence. It was consequently necessary to pay them a wage *before* the wages could be "reimbursed" by the sale of the products.

---

[1] We use the term risk here in its everyday sense, denoting the inherent uncertainty of the future; this uncertainty can be reduced by calculating probabilities, but it can never be completely eliminated.

H.C. Binswanger, *The Growth Spiral*, DOI 10.1007/978-3-642-31881-8_3,

Adam Smith called the capital needed to pay wages, together with the material to be worked up, the "wage fund." He wrote:

> As soon as stock has accumulated in the hands of particular persons, some of them will naturally employ it in setting to work industrious people, whom they will supply with materials and subsistence, in order to make a profit by the sale of their work, or by what their labor adds to the value of the materials. In exchanging the complete manufacture either for money, for labor, or for other goods, over and above what may be sufficient to pay the price of the materials and the wages of the workmen, something must be given for the profits of the undertaker of the work who hazards his stock in this adventure. . . . He could have no interest to employ them, unless he expected from the sale of their work something more than what was sufficient to replace his stock to him; and he could have no interest to employ a great stock rather than a small one, unless his profits were to bear some proportion to the extent of his stock. (WN I.vi, 5)

Although Adam Smith assumes that capital (stock) has to be saved up in one way or another, this entrepreneurial profit is never treated as reimbursing the act of saving, whether as a compensation for the discounting of future goods (the act of saving shifts consumption into the future) or as a reward for the restraint which the act of saving presupposes; it is only treated as compensation for the audacity or the risk, which is bound up with the investment of capital as an advance.[2]

The firm's profit can be divided between the net profit earned on equity capital and the interests paid to borrowed capital placed at the firm's disposal. Net profit is the part of profit that remains once the interest at a rate previously agreed has been paid on borrowed capital. This interest payment also has to be paid if there is no firm's profit, while net profit can only be secured if a profit has arisen. It is a residual. In the event of loss, which eventually leads to the inability to make payments and possibly to liquidation, borrowed capital can also be lost; that is the risk that it bears. But since the risk to equity capital is greater, the anticipated rate of profit that prompts the owner of equity capital to invest is normally higher than the rate of interest.

The classical conception of capital (stock) used here is totally different than the one that used in conventional economics. Here capital is understood to be "all means of production included in the production process, . . . such as tools, machines and buildings. 'Capital' consists therefore of goods that have been produced in previous production processes. . ." (Woll 1984, p. 54). In this sense capital is "real" (physical) capital, employed directly in production and which therefore appears as a factor of production. The payment of interest—in conventional economics there is

[2] Note a related argument by Hans von Mangoldt's (1824–1868) concerning the source of entrepreneurial profit or enterprise profit. Mangold is one of the few economists who were looking for an explanation of profit, rather than interest. Just like Adam Smith, he views profit as a compensation for risk. He states that according to "the nature of the enterprise, the entrepreneur bears the risks of production, i.e. he sells the products of his firm on his own account, while having personal responsibility for replacing the [real] capital used in production as well as for the payment of wages to his workers. Whatever surplus remains to him from this is the compensation for the sacrifice he has made, is therefore entrepreneurial profit" (von Mangoldt 1871, p. 35).

Note: This citation and all other non-English citations are translated by the author.

no mention of gain of profit so long as a condition of equilibrium is assumed—is treated as the price paid for the employment of "real" capital, analogous to the wages paid for the use of labor. As Adam Smith had pointed out,[3] this ignores the fact that the price of "real" capital, that is, the price of the means of production which have been produced, consists entirely of the prices of the factors of production with whose help they are produced, plus the price of money capital as an advance, making possible the production on the basis of the division of labor. From this it follows that no specific price, called "interest," can be imputed to "real" capital. Interest is, we repeat, a component of the firm's profit, a payment for the use of borrowed capital as an advance.

If produced means of production are used in addition to labor and materials, this just means that correspondingly more capital as an advance is needed: It is needed as a promotion factor, not only as variable capital as in Smith's wage fund but also as fixed capital which is used to purchase produced means of production and which is not used up in one production period but rather over the course of several periods. This itself ties up capital over a longer term.

So, I propose, that the word "capital" should generally be used in the classical sense understood by Adam Smith: as denoting the advance that firms need to initiate and continue production irrespective of whether it concerns variable or fixed capital and that profit and interest should only be attributed to capital conceived as an advance.

In this we agree with the view of Joseph Schumpeter, who emphasized that there is no reason

> . . .to distinguish between all the goods that the entrepreneur purchases, nor any reason to collect any one group of such goods together under the name "capital". . . . The capital of an enterprise is certainly not represented by all those goods that serve its ends. For capital is distinct from the world of goods: goods are purchased with capital—"capital is invested in goods"—but this involves the recognition that its function is distinct from that of the goods so acquired. The function of goods, depending on their technical nature, consists in serving a productive end, the technical and physical production of other goods. The function of capital consists in acquiring for the entrepreneur those goods that are productively employed, "set to work" we could say. Capital is the means for the acquisition of goods. . . . The entrepreneur has to have capital before he can start to think about acquiring actual

[3] Adam Smith argued on the basis of an agricultural enterprise organized around the use of capital, requiring draught animals and agricultural equipment that had to be bought from the leaseholder—the farmer—who made the capital available. He writes: "In the price of corn, for example, one part pays the rent of the landlord, another pays the wages or maintenance of the laborers and laboring cattle employed in producing it, and the third pays the profit of the farmer. These three parts seem either immediately or ultimately to make up the whole price of corn. A fourth part, it may perhaps be thought, is necessary for replacing the stock of the farmer, or for compensating the wear and tear of his laboring cattle, and other instruments of husbandry. But it must be considered that the price of any instrument of husbandry, such as a laboring horse, is itself made up of the same three parts; the rent of the land upon which he is reared, the labor of tending and rearing him, and the profits of the farmer who advances both the rent of this land, and the wages of this labor. Though the price of corn, therefore, may pay the price as well as the maintenance of the horse, the whole price still resolves itself either immediately or ultimately into the same three parts of rent, labor, and profit" (WN I.vi.11).

> goods. There is a point in time where he has the necessary capital but not yet the productive goods; and at this point one can see more clearly than at any other time that capital is not identical with concrete goods, but is instead an independent agent. And its sole purpose, the sole reason that the entrepreneur needs capital . . . is just that: to serve as a fund with which production goods can be paid for. (Schumpeter 1926, 167 f.)

Schumpeter poses the following question: What then is capital, if it consists neither in particular kind of goods or in goods in general?

> The answer is obvious enough: it is a fund of purchasing power. Only in this form can it fulfill its real function, the function for which capital is in practice alone necessary, and for which only the concept of capital has a theoretical application that cannot equally well be replaced by the designation of categories of goods. (Schumpeter 1926, p. 170)

And so, according to Schumpeter, interest payments are not made in respect of concrete goods (Schumpeter 1926, p. 261), but "have to flow from entrepreneurial profit" (Schumpeter 1926, p. 261). This recognition "puts an end to the constantly repeated efforts to locate a corresponding and lasting value component in concrete goods that relates to an interest payment" (Schumpeter 1926, p. 262).

While in Adam Smith's time it was still possible for the firm to pay worker's wages in goods, today the firm buys virtually all factors of production with money. It likewise sells all its products for money. Consequently, the capital needed as an advance has to be money, as has the firm's profit.

Karl Marx emphasized this point in the first volume of *Capital,* when he stated the formula for simple commodity circulation as

$$C - M - C,$$

where money M appears only to be the medium for exchange between commodities C. He expanded this formula to the "circulation of money as capital" as

$$M - C - M'.$$

In this case, enterprises use money as capital as an advance to purchase materials and factors of production, and with these produce commodities C, which they subsequently sell for M', a sum of money which is in excess of the advanced sum, so that

$$M' - M > 0.$$

The difference is the profit of the enterprises investing capital in order to produce commodities. Profit is therefore the surplus of money, which Marx explained as "surplus value" ("Mehrwert").[4]

[4] Marx's formulation is valid quite independently of whether his interpretation of surplus *money* as surplus *value* is valid. (For Marx's theory of surplus value, see p. 58 below.) It can be supposed that Marx drew on A. R. J. Turgot's (1727–1781) account of the "continuous advancing and return of capital." For Turgot capital is "useful and fruitful circulation that stimulates all labor in society" and "which maintains the movement and life of the body politic" (Turgot 1981, p. 201).

Marx's formula is the basis of every accounting, which task is to calculate the profit that is to be allocated to money capital.

The monetary form of profit was given special emphasis by Wilhelm Rieger, one of the founders of business economics: "The firm is an institution formed to realize a money income—here called profit—through its economic activity" (Rieger 1926, p. 44). From this it follows: "Since the firm calculates in money, and to the extent that it does so, profit is necessarily a monetary surplus" (Rieger 1926, p. 64).

His student Erich Preiser adopted this idea for general economics. He wrote:

> In practice capital is understood to be the means for financing investments, i.e., money for the purpose of investment; money in this function is capital... Rieger, with his incorruptible sense of reality, adopted a perspective on the economy as a whole and identified the essence of the capitalist firm as the application of a sum of money with the aim of increasing its amount. (Preiser 1961a, p. 105)[5]

The monetary orientation of the enterprise becomes even clearer if we recognize that normally the enterprise is a legal entity that comes into existence by having placed at its disposal money as capital. The beginning and the end of the firm is money. The real processes that take place in the firm are therefore for the management of the firm only of interest insofar as they are reflected in monetary results.

The instrument by which all magnitudes are converted into money values is double-entry bookkeeping. This instrument is essential for the enterprise. Double-entry accounting uses revenue and expenditure, or respectively plus and minus money values, to calculate the total balance sheet for the enterprise. This fact can be illustrated with a simple example, in which there are only labor costs (material costs being included in these) and no tax is paid.

Consider the activity of an enterprise over one year. It starts with its equity capital. This is entered as cash. With the sale of products money flows continually back into the cash account. The rate at which this happens depends both on the time needed to bring products to the market and on the temporal structure of the market process, where from one month to another more or less is sold. Because of this, some liquidity is needed as a buffer.[6] This means that the money which the provider of capital makes available in the form of money—the cash with which the enterprise initiates its activity—can in fact be smaller than the *annual* wage bill, but must be greater than the *monthly* wage bill.

We assume in our example that the costs on wages is 100 money units per month and so 1,200 money units per year, while the revenue over the course of the year is

[5] See also Johannes Schmidt (1998, 162 ff.).

[6] The relation of an enterprise to its cash balance differs considerably from that of a household. See the comment of Josef Ackermann (1977, p. 103): "To avoid problems of liquidity firms will throughout the production period retain a part of the cash that result from their transactions. ... Firms do not therefore collect all their money together so as to spend it during the following period. Instead, bills are also settled with money that has just been paid in. The problem of cash holdings, or of liquidity, is limited therefore to the clearing of net positions." The level of cash holdings is a matter of experience and judgment.

1,212 money units. At times, revenue can be smaller than costs. The enterprise therefore needs a reserve to ensure its liquidity, in our example at 20 money units.

The opening entries look like this[7].

	Debit	Credit
a. Cash	120	
Equity capital		120
b. Salary expense	1,200	
Cash		1,200
c. Cash	1,212	
Sales		1,212

ASSETS

Cash

a. 120	b. 1200
c. 1212	
Balance 132	

STOCKHOLDERS' EQUITY

Equity capital

	a. 120
	Balance 120

EXPENSES

Salary expense

b. 1200	
Balance 1200	

REVENUES

Sales

	c. 1212
	Balance 1212

At the end of the year, the accounts are reconciled and the balances are entered into the income statement and into the closing balance. The outcome of the income statement—the balance of all balances from the expenses and revenues accounts—is entered as profit into the income summary.

The closing entries run as follows:

	Debit	Credit
d. Income summary	1,200	
Salary expense		1,200
e. Sales	1,212	
Income summary		1,212

[7] The following account is simplified for the purpose of our example, which is a normal textbook procedure. I am indebted to Albert Gebhardt for the presentation of the three case-studies in accounting (see also pp. 32 and pp. 41).

Income summary

d.	1200	e.	1212
Net profit	12		
		Balance	0

EXPENSES
Salary expense

b.	1200		
		d.	1200
		Balance	0

REVENUES
Sales

		c.	1212
e.	1212		
Balance	0		

According to the income summary, the revenue from sales is 1,212 and salary expenses are 1,200. The balance is thus a net profit of 12. Relating this net profit of 12 to the equity capital of 120 results in a return on equity (ROE) of 10 %.

We assume that half of the net profit is paid to the provider of the equity capital. The remainder, 6 money units, is retained in the enterprise, so that the expansion of its activities can be autonomously financed, at least in part.

The corresponding closing entries are as follows:

	Debit	Credit
f. Income summary	12	
Distribution of profits		12
g. Distribution of profits	6	
Equity capital		6
h. Distribution of profits	6	
Cash		6

Distribution of profit

g.	6	f.	12
h.	6		
		Balance	0

ASSETS
Cash

a.	120	b.	1200
c.	1212	h.	6
Balance	126		

STOCKHOLDERS' EQUITY
Equity capital

		a.	120
		g.	6
		Balance	126

The balance sheet at the end of the year, which is compiled after the distribution of profits, looks as follows:

BALANCE SHEET

Assets		Liabilities & Stockholders' Equity	
Cash	126	Equity capital	126
Total	126	Total	126

This example demonstrates that in the final analysis, it is all about the balance of amounts of money, manifested either in a profit or a loss. Double-entry bookkeeping distils from the business activities of the firm a sum of money behind which real costs (in this case that of labor) and real revenue (in this case the quantity of goods produced) are simply "forgotten." It is only the amount of money gained which is crucial for the existence of the firm.

This realization of the firm in monetary terms flows from the fact that the creation of the firm is itself a monetary transaction—the "transmutation" of money into capital—and so the firm can only survive if the money that is expended continually flows back to it and in so doing increases, this increase being treated as a profit which at least equals the risk involved in the investment of capital and which in this way guarantees the continuous existence of the firm.

The household complements the firm. In contrast to the Walrasian individual economic unit that is in principle self-sufficient, the modern households receive a money wage from firms in payment for the labor or other production services they have put at their disposal and spend their income on the products made by firms. This means that households are bound up in the monetary framework related to the level of wages and the prices of products. In contrast with firms, the households are not concerned with the monetary balance of revenue and costs, but with the question of whether the wage, or more generally their revenue, is high enough to meet their wants, and they are also concerned that this revenue is spent in such a way that its use is optimized.

For households, therefore, double-entry bookkeeping, in which profit is recorded as a balance of balances, is of no relevance; instead, a simple recording of expenses is set off against revenues. Here the actual elements involved are "memorized." This may be made quite clear from an example of household accounting which has been put together from data taken from the Swiss index of consumer prices.

Household accounting			
Revenue		Expenses	
Income	100	Food and drink	14
		Clothing	5
		Housing and energy	26
		Housekeeping	5
		Health	13
		Travel and communication	11
		Leisure	11
		Restaurant and hotel	10
		Other	5
Total	100	Total	100

This kind of simple accounting is the means by which the household can judge how much it can spend. It serves as a check on the limits of its spending, so that it remains within its given budget constraint. It governs the household's behavior quite independently of how effectively this is done or whether it is done more in the mind than in a written form. The entries not only have a meaning as information on the level of money costs but also indicate the goods upon which this cost is laid out. These are assessed by the household for their utility, in terms of the extent to which they satisfy real wants.

If its basic needs are not met, the household ceases to exist. The household as a reality therefore depends upon the real use of the products, which it is able to consume. It will consequently, if it calculates rationally, demand exactly that amount of each product in such a way that with declining marginal utility the final unit of money expended on a product creates for all products the same marginal utility. Decisive are the household's preferences.

The profit orientation of firms complements the orientation of households to real goods and services. Firms have to keep an eye on the real wants of households so that they are able to sell their products to households, and the households have to earn money by selling their factors of production to firms for money, so that they can in turn buy products from the firms. This interconnection of monetary and real wants is the basis of the market process.[8]

3.2 The Market as a Dynamic Process

Relative prices are only of secondary importance in the market. Money or absolute prices determine which good will be supplied or demanded in greater quantity and which in lesser quantity for they not only give information on the relative prices, which can be calculated retrospectively from the comparison of money prices, but also determine whether firms achieve a profit or whether they suffer a loss, whether they begin production, and whether they continue to produce, close down, or can expand. The market is a process that is driven on with the help of money or absolute prices and the prospect of monetary gain or monetary loss.

To construct a model corresponding to this drive, we turn to the law of supply and demand that Adam Smith presented in his book *The Wealth of Nations*. He presents the market process in terms of the interaction of firms and households, producers and consumers. His account must be distinguished from the neoclassical model based on Walras by virtue of the way that Smith builds time into his framework.[9]

[8] If we assume that firms and households behave as "homines oeconomici"—firms maximizing profit, households maximizing utility—this should not be read too rigorously. Both have some scope to orient their decisions on production and consumption to some other end, such as ethical or ecological criteria. But firms have less free play than households, since profit is determined monetarily both on the costs and the revenue side. For households this is only true on the costs side. See for a discussion of the significance of free play in firms and households Peter Ulrich (1997) as well as Helge Peukert (2005) on ethical aspects and Thomas Dyllick, Frank Belz, and Uwe Scheidewind (1997) and Volker Stahlmann (1994, 201 ff.) on environmental aspects. The different forms of the "homo oeconomicus" are discussed by Gebhard Kirchgässner (1997, 2000).

[9] Here we base our account of the classical theory on the work of Bertram Schefold (1981a, b) and Ernst Helmstädter (1981). We are not so much concerned here with issues of Adam Smith interpretation, but wish rather to develop the simplest possible representation of the market process involving the temporal path of the market process.

Smith starts out from the inversion of sale → purchase into purchase → sale that arises from the use of capital as an advance. To demonstrate this, we choose an industrial firm that needs only labor and material. First of all labor and material is bought, products are made with their help, and then subsequently the products are sold on the market. To make clear the necessity of the use of capital, we have to distinguish between a period in which production takes place—the production period—and a period in which the goods produced are brought to the market—the market period. During the production period, the worker lives of wage payments that come from the advanced money, that is, from capital. It is in Adam Smith's terms the "wage fund." During the market period, the capital that has been employed is supposed to flow back through the sale of the goods together with a profit.

To understand the functioning of the market, it is important to take account of the fact that the firm does not know when its starts the production process, which quantity, and at which price it will be able to sell its goods when they arrive at the market. It produces for unknown consumers who decide on a purchase only when the goods are in front of them. The consumers arrive at this decision on the basis of ever-changing preferences and taking into account their income that is also subject to variation. This means that the prices that arise from the meeting of supply with demand during the market period are influenced by changing preferences and income conditions of the consumer.

We can therefore establish the following principles. The capital employed in the firm bears a risk. Capital demands compensation for this in the form of a minimum profit which is made up of the minimum net profit of the shareholder and the rate of interest agreed with the providers of borrowed capital. The money price realized in the market has therefore to cover over and above the production costs the anticipated minimum or "normal" profit, so that capital is not withdrawn to try its luck elsewhere. Only if the minimum profit is realized, a continuous process of reproduction of the goods concerned occurs.[10]

Adam Smith calls the price that allows for a minimum profit over and above production costs the "natural price." We will call this price the reproduction price, that is, the price which secures the continuation of the production process.[11] From this it follows that the market price (p) must at least cover the reproduction price (p^{r}), so that production can be continued, as in

$$p \geq p^{\mathrm{r}}$$

[10] The classical conception of the market price which is supposed to cover at least the minimum "normal" profit is dealt with by Spahn in his "Macroeconomics." In his words, "The decision to start production is bound up with the expectation that the usual market return on equity and borrowed capital can be made through the prices at which the goods are sold in the market. The minimum profit is included in the calculation of the product price" (Spahn 1999, p. 31).

[11] This identification of "natural price" with the "reproduction price" is taken from Heinz D. Kurz and Neri Salvadori: "The prices of reproduction ... were conceived as expressing the persistent, non-accidental and non-temporary forces governing the economic system, and were thus distinguished from 'actual' or 'market' prices, which reflected all kinds of influences, many of an accidental and temporary nature" (Kurz and Salvadori 1995, 1 f.).

in which
p^{r} = reproduction price
= production costs strictly speaking + anticipated minimum profit (minimum net profit + interest payment)
= costs of reproduction

To present the dynamics of the market process, we make use of the classical two-period model. In the first period, production takes place, and in the second, the goods produced are offered in the market. Period t is the production period in which quantity $\bar{q}_t^{\mathrm{p}}$ is produced. In period $t+1$ it comes to the market and, leaving aside warehousing, it becomes supply $\bar{q}_{t+1}$, so that

$$\bar{q}_{t+1} = \bar{q}_t^{\mathrm{p}}.$$

For the sake of simplicity, it is assumed, just as in the model of Smith, that the average production costs are independent of the quantity produced (but this is not an assumption that is absolutely necessary). We assume also a falling demand curve on the basis of empirical experience.

The firms set the level of production with regard to the demand at the reproduction price p_t^{r} that they anticipate for the following period. Such anticipations can be disappointed, either positively or negatively, since demand can change from one period to another. The market price p_{t+1} can therefore deviate from the reproduction price p_t^{r}.

Two cases have to be distinguished:

(a) Supply $\bar{q}_{t+1} (= \bar{q}_t^{\mathrm{p}})$ is less than the market demand at price p_t^{r}, that is, less than $q_{t+1}(p_t^{\mathrm{r}})$, and so

$$\bar{q}_{t+1} < q_{t+1}(p_t^{\mathrm{r}}).$$

In this case, the market price p_{t+1} lies above the reproduction price p_t^{r}; hence,

$$p_{t+1} > p_t^{\mathrm{r}}.$$

This relationship is shown in Fig. 3.1.

At the reproduction price p_t^{r}, the entire demand cannot be met. There is a surplus demand of

$$q_{t+1}(p_t^{\mathrm{r}}) - \bar{q}_{t+1} = q_{t+1}(p_t^{\mathrm{r}}) - \bar{q}_t^{\mathrm{p}}.$$

The consumers compete among themselves for the insufficient supply, driving the market price upward. In this way, the surplus profit per unit is equal to

$$p_{t+1} - p_t^{\mathrm{r}}.$$

(b) Supply $\bar{q}_{t+1} (= \bar{q}_t^{\mathrm{p}})$ is greater than market demand at price p_t^{r}, that is, than $q_{t+1}(p_t^{\mathrm{r}})$, and so

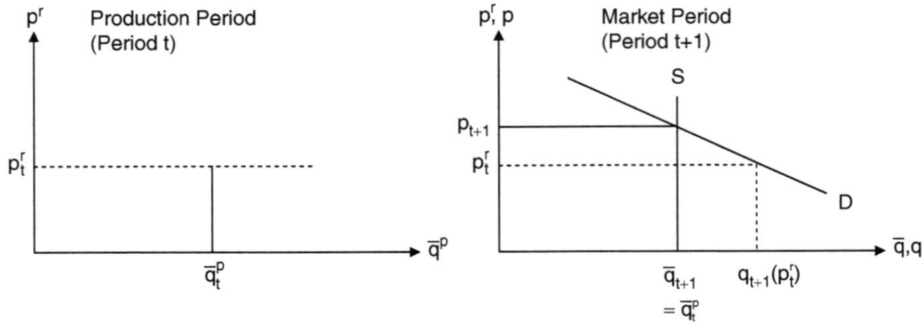

Fig. 3.1 The formation of market price under excess demand

$$\bar{q}_{t+1} > q_{t+1}\left(p_t^{\mathrm{r}}\right).$$

In this case the market price p_{t+1} lies below the reproduction price p_t^{r}; hence,

$$p_{t+1} < p_t^{\mathrm{r}}.$$

This relationship is shown in Fig. 3.2.

At the reproduction price p_t^{r}, the entire supply cannot be sold. There is an excess supply of

$$\bar{q}_{t+1} - q_{t+1}\left(p_t^{\mathrm{r}}\right) = \bar{q}_t^{\mathrm{p}} - q_{t+1}\left(p_t^{\mathrm{r}}\right).$$

Firms compete with each other for the insufficient demand, reducing the market price. There is a "loss" per unit of

$$p_t^{\mathrm{r}} - p_{t+1}.$$

This "loss" can also consist of a lesser profit, hence a profit smaller than the anticipated "normal" profit. Risk is then inadequately compensated.

If expectations are not fulfilled, either too little or too much being produced and consequently a surplus profit or "loss" being registered, Smith argues that a trial-and-error process commences that can last for several periods, the reproduction price acting as a magnet pushing the market price up or pulling it down.

At the end of this process, the market price equals the reproduction price; hence, $p_{t+1} = p_t^{\mathrm{r}}$.

If this is the case, the production is $\bar{q}_t^{\mathrm{p}}$, and so the supply to the market is $\bar{q}_{t+1}$ equals the quantity $q_{t+1}\left(p_t^{\mathrm{r}}\right)$ demanded in the market. This in turn equals the so-called effective demand q_t^{e}, which the supplier had assumed when planning production at time t. The long-run equilibrium is then

$$\bar{q}_t^{\mathrm{p}} = \bar{q}_{t+1} = q_{t+1}\left(p_t^{\mathrm{r}}\right) = q_t^{\mathrm{e}}.$$

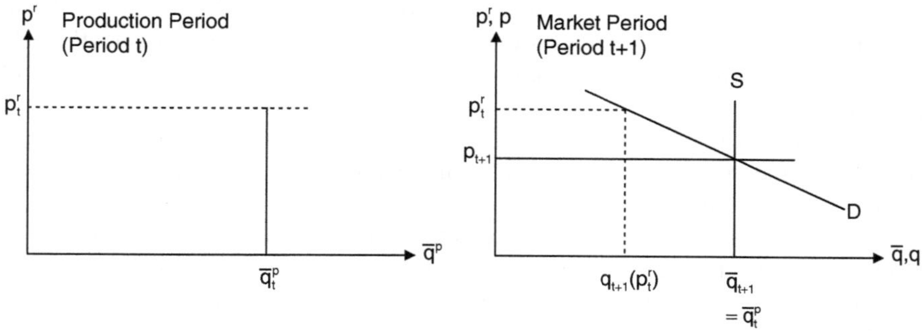

Fig. 3.2 The formation of market price under excess supply

The market is in this way "regulated" by "the law of supply and demand" in such a way that over time production eventually adapts to effective demand.[12]

In this long-run equilibrium, a "normal profit" arises as a part of the reproduction price.

But the trial-and-error process in the market opens up also a quite different perspective from that provided by the temporal adaptation of production to the effective demand under given conditions. Rather, it gives the firm the opportunity to understand competition as the challenge to alter these conditions in such a way that this adaptation does *not* come about, so that there is no long-run equilibrium. This means that that competition is treated by the firm as a chance to create new competitive advantages and so to increase profits. The claim to compensation for taking on the risk of production becomes in this way a constant tendency for a further maximization of profit. There is no reason to pause in the path to increasing profits once one has taken it! Success depends on the skill of the entrepreneur in taking advantage of opportunities as they arise. The fact that each firm has to assume that already existing or potential competitors will proceed in the same way, every firm has to fear a loss in the market share and so a shrinking of its profit below the reproduction costs. If this happens, it would lead to the withdrawal of capital and eventually to bankruptcy or liquidation. The striving for the maximization of profit is therefore not solely motivated by the search for "more" but also by the avoidance of "less."[13]

The firms can survive the pressure of competition by using restrictive strategies or by developing expansive strategies.

---

[12] This process can be clarified mathematically by a difference equation model. See Ernst Helmstädter (1981, 100 ff.).

[13] See on this Wolfgang Stolper: "Equilibrium theory describes processes of adaptation. But this is only one part of the capitalist economy. There is no explanation of why equilibrium is repeatedly disturbed by the *logic of the system* itself. Contrary to the assumptions of equilibrium theory, production functions change under endogenous impulses. Entrepreneurs actively *search* for new opportunities for profit if the older sources are eroded" (Stolper 1994, 20 f.).

Restrictive strategies involve the creation of barriers to market entry. As Adam Smith recognized, these strategies enable market prices to be permanently held above prices of reproduction. Natural or artificial monopolies or cartels are of assistance in this. Another possibility is the securing of government contracts.

Expansionary strategies have two different objectives: raising capacity while at the same time reducing costs (process innovation) or inventing new products (product innovation).[14]

Cost reduction makes it possible to reduce price without the reduction in costs being fully reflected in this reduced price as long it is possible to sell a greater quantity. So, the innovatory firm makes a dual gain: by increasing both the profit margin per unit and the quantity of units sold.

The *invention of new products* makes it possible to attract additional potential demand by stimulating new wants. It is important to present the products in such a manner that at least in one phase of the product life cycle, the elasticity demand is less than with conventional products. Then, the profit margin increases.[15]

Since the industrial revolution, expansionist strategies based on innovation have dominated. We owe to Friedrich Hayek the idea of competition as a "discovery procedure" and hence "the absurdity of the usual presumption" that all relevant circumstances are assumed to be known—"a situation which theory, strange to say, calls perfect competition, but in which there is no longer any possibility for the *activity* which we associate with competition" (Hayek 2003, p. 137).

---

[14] Adam Smith also dealt with expansionary strategies, although not in the context of the explanation of the market process but in the context of the explanation of the division of labor and his advantages, underlining the significance of competition. George B. Richardson states: "Smith offers us in effect both a theory of equilibrium and a theory of economic evolution and in each of it competition has a key role to play" (Richardson 1975, p. 351). Andrea Lavezzi adds: "We argue that the process of growth envisaged by Smith has essentially the nature of a disequilibrium process supported by competition" (Lavezzi 2003, p. 87).

[15] From this perspective, it becomes clear that the entrepreneur plays a central role in *ongoing* market process and is not restricted to innovation as a special case, as Joseph Schumpeter claimed. Although he emphasized the role of entrepreneur like no other modern writer, he failed to see that the role of the entrepreneur has more significance than he allowed to it. This failure originated from his allegiance to the Walrasian model of general equilibrium, in which the entrepreneur has no real function, as Walras himself recognized. Schumpeter consequently defines the entrepreneur as a personality who "realises new combinations, opens up new markets for it, and enters into direct conflict with competitors" (Schumpeter 1926, p. 174). But, if the entrepreneur runs the firm "statically" without further innovation, then "he ceases to be an entrepreneur. The character of the entrepreneur is related to the creation of the new" (Schumpeter 1926, p. 174). Hence, it is in his view also correct "that the entrepreneur," and for Schumpeter, this means also the firm as such, "receives nothing in a static situation" (Schumpeter 1926, p. 175), which means that the normal profit is zero. Schumpeter explains this by the fact that "the combination of factors of production in that situation is already determined, they are a legacy, and so there is nothing for the entrepreneur to do apart from routine matters, which means by extension that he receives nothing for this routine activity" (Schumpeter 1926, p. 175). The identification of the ongoing process of production and sales with a routine process prevents Schumpeter from seeing that the entrepreneur has to take permanently decisions on a daily basis relating to sales that involve a perpetual risk. He has therefore *constantly* to defend himself against such risks.

Fig. 3.3 The determination of the price of a good *j* under partial equilibrium

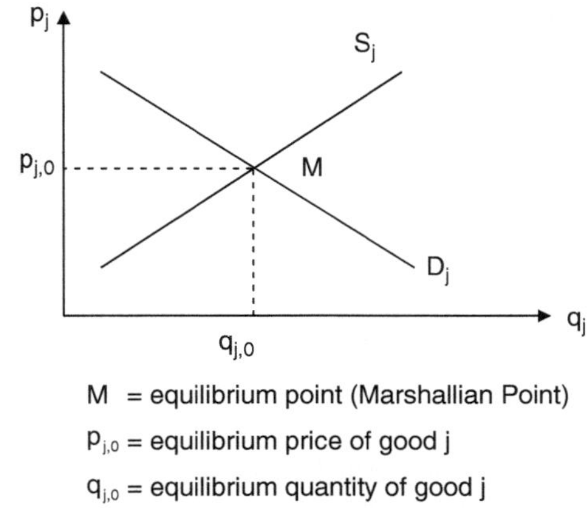

The manner in which time is embedded in the classical theory of supply and demand contrasts not only with the theory of general equilibrium but also with the theory of partial equilibrium found in the conventional textbooks. This theory can be traced back to Alfred Marshall's reformulation of supply and demand in his book *Principles of Economics*. Marshall believed that he had bridged the gap between the classical theory of Adam Smith and Ricardo and the neoclassical theory of Walras, firstly by replacing the concept of a general market equilibrium with a concept of equilibrium of a market for each individual product and secondly by replacing the concept of fixed supply with one in which supply increases as the money price rises.

It was in this way that the well-known "scissors" model of price determination came about, the falling demand curve and the rising supply curve for which the price was determined at the point that they intersect. Marshall explained:

> The "cost of production principle" and the "final utility" principle are undoubtedly component parts of the one over-ruling law of supply and demand; each may be compared to one blade of a pair of scissors. When one blade is held still, and the cutting is effected by moving the other, we may say with careless brevity that the cutting is done by the second. (Marshall 1961, I, p. 820)

The point of intersection of the supply and demand curves is the equilibrium point M, which was later called the Marshallian Point. It shows the price at which the quantities supplied and demanded are equal (see Fig. 3.3).

Marshall wanted to harmonize classical and neoclassical theory with this model. He assumed that the difference between the two theories only results from different assumptions about the position of the supply curve.

If supply is fixed, and so the supply curve is vertical, it is only demand and hence the level of demand D that determines the market price (see Fig. 3.4).

The price p_2 is in this case exactly as much above price p_1 as the demand curve D_2 is above the demand curve D_1.

Fig. 3.4 Price determination with a vertical supply curve

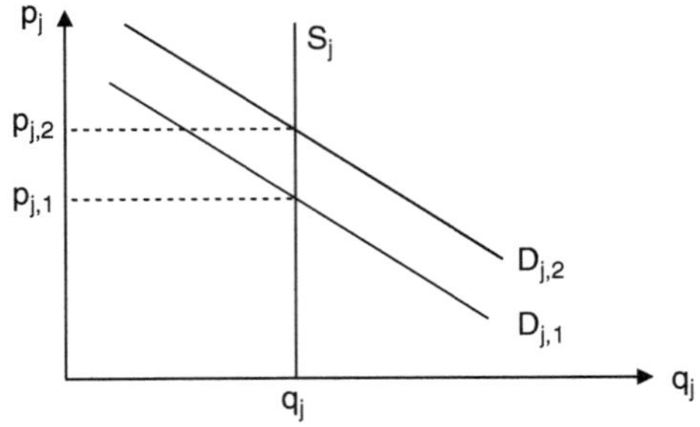

Fig. 3.5 Price determination with a horizontal supply curve

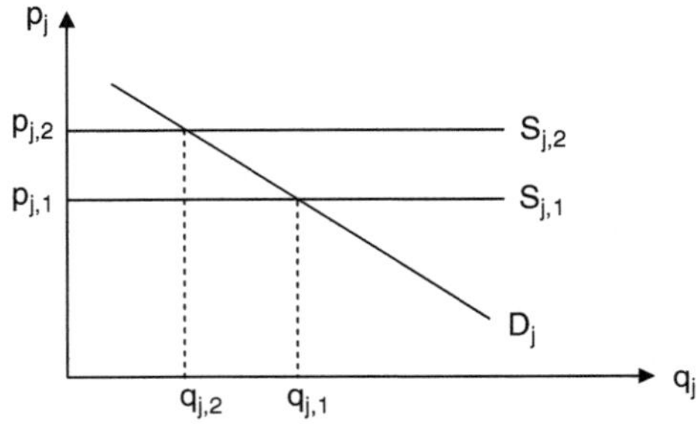

If however the costs of production are given and constant, such that the supply curve is horizontal, it is only supply and hence the level of production costs that determines the market price (see Fig. 3.5).

The price p_2 is in this case as much above the price p_1 as the supply curve S_2 is above the supply curve S_1.

Marshall believed that he had synthesized the classical and neoclassical theories into a new whole in which they became simply two extremities of a general case. The general case is for him represented by the upwardly sloping supply curve, and the downward sloping demand curve, and thus the determination of market price by utility *and* costs, as in Fig. 3.3.

But this synthesis remained incomplete, for Marshall did not grasp the decisive difference between the two theories. This difference does not come from the form of the supply curve, but rather from the Walrasian explanation of market price without taking into account the time dimension of the market process, whereas time plays a significant role in the classical theory. In the Walrasian model, products are offered for sale at the same instant that they are produced. In the classical model, production precedes supply in the market.

If one takes account of this difference, then it can be seen that the Marshallian approach is based upon the Walrasian and not on the classical theory. In the theory of partial equilibrium, production and supply are taking place at the same time, just as in the theory of general equilibrium, and belong therefore to the atemporal theory of Walras.

This explains why it is necessary to return to the classical theory of supply and demand, not only to replace the theory of general equilibrium but also to replace the theory of partial equilibrium.

3.3 Fixed and Variable Capital: The Inclusion of Produced Means of Production in the Production Process and the Impact on the Legal Form of the Firm

Produced means of production in the form of tools have always been used in the production process. However, their significance was still in the beginning of the eighteenth century so small that they were simply treated as aids to labor, without giving them any particular place in economic theory. This changed when machines—energy-powered tools—started to be used. The first machines appeared in the middle of the eighteenth century around the time of Adam Smith. But the financial means necessary to use them were so insignificant that Smith could more or less ignore them and treat capital chiefly as the "wage fund" used to pay for labor and materials. Subsequently, the share of machines in the production process has been increasing, and capital became subdivided into variable capital more or less identical with the "wage fund" on the one hand and fixed capital on the other.

We must therefore in the modern economy distinguish between these two forms of capital. This is because produced means of production are slow to repay their cost of purchase, each annual write-off being only a fraction of the original cost of purchase. Consequently, the increased mechanization of production implied an enormous increase in the need for advanced money, that is, capital, which in turn made necessary the introduction of borrowed capital alongside equity capital. The borrowed capital comes primarily from banks which advance credits or loans against the payment of interest. They have the advantage of being cheap, since a rate of interest are fixed and so interest payments remain low even when higher profits are earned. But the disadvantage is that the loans have to be eventually paid back, and interest payments still have to be made even if no profit is made. The banks therefore make sure that their credits were linked to the increase of the firm's equity capital, so that the risk is primarily born by the shareholder.

But also the risk of the shareholder is restricted. He does not have to risk his entire property, but only a limited sum. Liability is restricted to the amount of subscribed shares. The large sums of equity capital that are needed to finance the installation of machines, etc., can thus come from the collection of small capital contributions. In reality, the share is nothing more than a nonreturnable credit which has variable interest payments, instead of a fixed one. Johannes Rüegg-Stürm rightly states in his book *Controlling für Manager*: "Shareholders have no legal claim to interest payments. Nonetheless, the annual net profit is really the interest payment with which invested equity capital is remunerated" (Rüegg-Stürm 1996, p. 60).

The extension of the firm through the inclusion of produced means of production and the resulting consequences for the organization and management of the firm can be seen in the accounts of a joint stock company which employs machines, etc., and which uses borrowed capital alongside equity capital. This can be explained in an example beginning with the year when machines, etc., are purchased for the first time.

To keep things simple, we include cost of the materials and the energy into wages. The firm purchases labor, materials, and energy from households and machines from other firms.

The amount of cash in the opening balance has to be sufficiently large to pay for the machines that are purchased. The sale of goods creates a revenue stream. Wages can to a great extent be paid from the revenue that flows in from the sale of products. Consequently, as we have already seen in the example of the firm which only has wage costs, wage payments can be less than the *annual* wage bill, even if it is at a higher level than the *monthly* wage bill. In our example, the greater part of the firm's capital is equity capital, with a smaller amount of borrowed capital.

Besides the payments for labor and equipments (machinery etc.), interest payments have to be made. In contrast to the payments on labor and equipment, interest payments are made only at year's end from the return on capital, so that no cash has to be set aside for them at the beginning of the period. The decisive distinction between the accounts of a firm without machines and the accounts of one with machines is that the value of the machinery (net of depreciation) is shown in the closing balance as assets of the firm.

Our example runs as follows: The firm begins its business activity with a total capital of 6,000 money units, of which 4,000 money units are equity capital and 2,000 money units are borrowed capital (loan debt). At the opening of business, the assets consist entirely of the cash balance (equal to the total of liquid assets). The opening balance can be represented as follows.

BALANCE SHEET

Assets		Liabilities & Stockholders' Equity		
Cash	6000	Loan debt	(borrowed capital)	2000
		Equity capital		4000
Total	6000	Total		6000

We assume that during the year, salary expenses in the amount of 9,900 money units have to be made. In addition, equipment (machinery etc.) is bought for 5,000 money units. It is assumed that the machine will be employed for a period of 10 years. Depreciation is linear, which gives a depreciation rate of 10 % of the original value. The interest rate on borrowed capital is 5 %. The revenue from sales is 11,500 units.

This is entered as follows:

	Debit	Credit
a. Salary expense	9,900	
Cash		9,900
b. Equipment	5,000	
Cash		5,000
c. Cash	11,500	
Sales		11,500
d. Interest expense	100	
Cash		100
e. Depreciation	500	
Equipment		500

ASSETS

Cash

Balance	6000	a.	9900
c.	11500	b.	5000
		d.	100
Balance	2500		

Equipment

b.	5000	e.	500
Balance	4500		

REVENUES

Sales

		c.	11500
		Balance	11500

EXPENSES

Salary expense

a.	9900		
Balance	9900		

Interest expense

d.	100		
Balance	100		

Depreciation

e.	500		
Balance	500		

The closing entries and the corresponding entries in the income summary are as follows:

	Debit	Credit
f. Sales	11,500	
Income summary		11,500
g. Income summary	9,900	
Salary expense		9,900
h. Income summary	100	
Interest expense		100
i. Income summary	500	
Depreciation		500

Income summary

Debit		Credit	
g.	9900	f.	11500
h.	100		
i.	500		
Net profit	1000		
		Balance	0

REVENUES

Sales

Debit		Credit	
f.	11500	c.	11500
Balance	0		

EXPENSES

Salary expense

Debit		Credit	
a.	9900	g.	9900
		Balance	0

Interest expense

Debit		Credit	
d.	100	h.	100
		Balance	0

Depreciation

Debit		Credit	
e.	500	i.	500
		Balance	0

The net profit of the firm is 1,000 money units or 25 % of equity capital.

If we assume that half of the firm's profit is paid out as dividends to the providers of equity and that the other half is being retained in the firm and used to increase the equity capital, then the following entries can be made.

	Debit	Credit
j. Income summary	1,000	
Distribution of profits		1,000
k. Distribution of profits	500	
Equity capital		500
l. Distribution of profits	500	
Cash		500

Distribution of profit

Debit		Credit	
k.	500	j.	1000
l.	500		
		Balance	0

ASSETS

Cash

Debit		Credit	
Balance	6000	a.	9900
c.	11500	b.	5000
		d.	100
		l.	500
Balance	2000		

STOCKHOLDERS' EQUITY

Equity capital

Debit		Credit	
			4000
		k.	500
		Balance	4500

The balance sheet at the end of the year looks as follows:

BALANCE SHEET

Assets		Liabilities & Stockholders' Equity	
Cash	2000	Loan debt (borrowed capital)	2000
Equipment	4500	Equity capital	4500
Total	6500	Total	6500

We can state the outcome of the use of machinery in the production process as follows: Equity capital has increased by 500 money units. The providers of the equity capital, the shareholders, have received 500 money units as their share of the profits. With the investment of 4,000 units of equity capital, this corresponds to a dividend of 12.5 %.

But the crucial point is that cash holdings have shrunk from 6,000 units to 2,000 due to the purchase of real assets (equipment). The linear depreciation on the other side reduces the amount paid for the equipment (5,000) by 10 % causing an end of year balance of 4,500. The annual profit of the firm is thus no longer equal to the difference between income and cash outgoings, but equal to the difference between asset gains and asset losses. As a consequence, there is a new liquidity risk, since the equipment stock of 4,500 money units can only be liquidated with difficulty, if at all. It can therefore be possible, that despite profits being made, there is not enough cash to meet outstanding obligations.

Shortages of liquidity are chiefly a problem if the share of borrowed capital is high. The liquidity risk can however be reduced if the amount of equity capital is increased, whether by a new share issue or by retaining and reinvesting part of the profit, proportionally to the increase of borrowed capital. The reinvestment of a part of the profit involves the prospect of higher profits in the future and hence an increase in share value. Investment means that the firm grows. But this growth does increase the risk of a liquidity shortage in the future, since its equipment stock increases again. However, the future can be postponed indefinitely by repeatedly retaining profits and reinvesting these retained profits. Thus, a growth strategy can continuously reduce the risk of a liquidity shortage, while increasing profits.

This example confirms once again that money is the true reality for a firm. But it is no longer just a matter of the relation between the profit registered in the closing balance and the equity recorded in the opening balance; it is also a question of the liquidity situation, the relationship between cash and fixed assets. Maintenance of liquidity as well as consideration of the profits pushes production toward growth.

Machines and other equipment are produced means of production and as such themselves industrial products. The sector of industry that specializes in their production is called investment goods industry, which, of course, also produces for itself. Its purpose is however the delivery of machinery and other equipment to the consumer goods industry. The production of investment goods has to occur before the consumer goods industry can purchase investment goods and install them.

The market for investment goods is different from that for consumer goods as outlined above. Investment goods are generally not mass produced, but are oriented to the specific needs of the user. They are as a consequence produced to order. In consequence, firms producing investment goods bear no market risk. They are in fact bought before they are produced. The risk here is born by the firms producing consumer goods that the investment good which they have ordered, and for which payment in full normally falls due on delivery, will never be fully used. Yet, the investment goods industry bears also a risk. This is because investment goods have no strictly determined technical lifetime; thus, the time of their replacement can vary according to the market outlook or other cyclical factors. Orders for investment goods are therefore subject to great swings, and these can cause their makers great problems if they carry high fixed costs, which is usually the case. Accordingly, the investment goods industry is even more reliant on constant economic growth than the consumer goods industry, for in a growing economy the consumer goods industry will continually renew investment goods and so renew their orders with according to the increase of their production.

Money and Money Creation in a Two-Stage Banking System

4

4.1 The Increase of the Money Supply by the Creation of Money through Credit

The displacement of barter economy by the monetary economy required a continuous increase in the quantity of money according to the increase of trade and production. As long as money was just pieces of silver and gold, the quantity of money could only be increased by digging up more gold and silver. The rate of increase was very low. This first changed with the discovery of the Americas, resulting in a flood of gold and silver which, via Spain and Portugal, spread throughout Europe, chiefly to France, the Netherlands, and England. Prices rose, and there was also a demand for ever greater amounts of money, since the influx of gold and silver coins had stimulated trade and commerce, whose growth in turn depended on increasing amounts of coins. Therefore, the coinage was often debased creating alloys of gold and silver with less valuable metals. But this brought great disorder to the monetary system.

The discrepancy between the strong demand for money and the limited possibilities of increasing its quantity was overcome at the end of the seventeenth century by the introduction of paper money.

The decisive step was the foundation in 1692 of the Bank of England, which from 1696 on issued bank notes. At the same time, Britain adopted gold coin as the standard currency, lending the new system stability despite—or because—of the fact that intrinsically valueless paper money circulated alongside gold coins. It was sufficient that the paper money could be converted 1:1 into gold coins. In fact only a small amount of paper money was cashed in, since it was always possible to make payments with the new paper money. The issue of bank notes was later supplemented by bank money based on the creation of sight deposits at commercial banks on the giro or checking accounts, which could be exchanged 1:1 for paper money. The commercial banks obtained paper money, which in the meantime had become legal tender, from the Bank of England, either against gold or credit. But the bank could offer commercial banks only a limited amount of paper money on

H.C. Binswanger, *The Growth Spiral*, DOI 10.1007/978-3-642-31881-8_4,

credit so long as this paper money was convertible into gold coins. The level of the Bank of England's gold reserves therefore represented a limitation on the creation of bank money. Despite this, the quantity of money expanded enormously.

This dual banking system—a central bank issuing bank notes and commercial banks giving credits in form of sight deposits, that is, as bank money—was in time adopted throughout the world.

In 1931 England put an end to the obligation to convert paper money into gold on demand, and the rest of the world eventually followed suit. One small element of the gold standard remained, in that a central bank was still obliged to settle debts with another central bank in gold. Ultimately, when the International Monetary Fund was formed in 1946, it was considered sufficient that central bank debts be covered in US dollars and that only the US dollar was convertible into gold. This obligation was itself unilaterally terminated by the USA in 1973. This had been the final end of the gold standard regime.

Since then, we have a monetary system that is based ultimately on paper money, that is, bank notes of the central banks, or on sight deposits of the commercial banks, that is, bank money, that can be converted into bank notes on demand. But banks notes can no longer be exchanged for gold at a rate of 1:1. They became definitive (final) money. Flexible exchange rates between national currencies have replaced the obligation to meet the debts of one central bank with another in gold. This flexible exchange rate regime, together with intervention of the International Monetary Fund (IMF), should ideally prevent any debts arising between central banks.

This abolished in principle all restrictions on the increase of the quantity of money. And so money seems to come from nowhere. Consequently one talks of money creation, analogously with the creation of the world, which also came from nowhere.[1]

Today the producers of money are in the first instance the commercial banks and not the central banks (for the sake of convenience, we will henceforth refer to commercial banks simply as "banks"). All newly created money—with the exception of the advance of emergency credit to the state by the central bank—is principally bank money. Monetary creation is therefore part—the most important part—of the business activity of a bank. As Henry Dunning MacLeod rightly stated, "A bank . . . is not an office for borrowing and lending money, but it is a manufactory of credit" (MacLeod 1889, p. 93). Joseph Schumpeter wrote in a similar vein: "Credit is really the creation of purchasing power for the purpose of transferring this to the entrepreneur, and not the transfer of existing purchasing power to him" (Schumpeter 1926, p. 153). Augusto Graziani supplements this statement of Schumpeter, based upon his "circulation approach":

[1] On the controversies related to the creation of money, see Bernd Senf (2005, pp. 88–110).

> The circulation approach rejects the idea that deposits make loans, an idea that Schumpeter already considered an old prejudice. In the circulation approach the opposite conception is adopted, namely that loans make deposits. The "old prejudice" is based on the assumption that, without a previous collection of deposits, the banking system would be unable to make any loan since, when making loans, a bank makes use of previously collected deposits. Simple considerations of banking technique show the inconsistency of this idea. An agent opening a bank deposit doesn't lose his own liquidity, since he is able to make use of his deposit as a means of payment at any moment and without notice. At the same time a bank, when making a new loan, is granting additional liquidity to an agent without subtracting any liquidity to any of its own depositors. Therefore . . ., when a bank makes a loan to a customer, it is not transmitting liquidity from one agent to another one but creating new liquidity. (Graziani 2003, 82f)

Schumpeter's "purchasing power" and Graziani's "liquidity" are what we call bank money.

Banks are firms which—like all firms—sell their products in the market for profit. Money is a market product like any other. Money is also produced for the purpose of making profits.

Bank money is created when banks grant credit and book these credits into sight deposits of the borrowers, or those who receive payments from such borrowers. Sight deposits are debts of the bank owed to the account holder and so represent a credit granted by the account holder to the bank. Thus, bank money in the form of sight deposits is created by a relationship involving dual debts and dual credits: The credit extended by the bank to borrowers is matched by credit extended by the holder of a credit balance to the bank. And so commercial banks extend credits by incurring debts. As Richard Sayers commented, the borrower pays his debts with bank debts.[2]

The trick in money creation is that the credit granted by the account holder to the bank in form of sight deposits does not appear to be a debt, because the debt changes into bank money. This is even a superior form of money since it makes payment easier; a payment can be authorized in writing or electronically and has not to be passed from hand to hand. Consequently the holders of sight deposits demand no interest payment—or if so, at a very low rate—for the credit which they grant the bank.

The capacity of commercial banks to create money is limited only by the small part of sight deposits they have to hold with the central bank as a reserve. The banks have to hold central bank money in a certain relationship to sight deposits on the liability account in their balance sheet, whereby this relationship is determined

[2] "Banks are institutions whose debts—usually referred to as 'bank deposits'—are commonly accepted in final settlement of other people's debts." R. Sayers (1964, p. 1)

both by the custom and practice of the bank, as well as by regulations regarding minimum reserves.[3]

The crucial point is however that the central bank can always provide additional money to the banks, which they need as a reserve, mostly by repurchase agreements which can be interpreted as credits to the banks. Central bank money, whether bank notes or sight deposits held by the banks on the liability account in the balance sheet of the central bank, is on the other side a debt of the central bank, because originally they had to be redeemed in gold. But since the obligation to do so was abolished, this debt has become not only de facto but de jure "eternal." For this reason the central bank can present act *always* as "lender of last resort," if the banks need additional reserves.

As with all firms, banks need also equity capital at their disposal. Equity capital "requires" profit as compensation for the risk of financing business activities. But the risks are different for firms which produce goods and for banks. In the production of goods, this risk is formed chiefly by the time lag between the production and the market period, because at the time that goods are produced one does not know whether they can subsequently be sold at a price that meets the costs of production. There is by contrast in the production—the creation—of money by granting credits no such time lag between the production and the market period. Production and sale occur at the same time. The price in the form of interest can be agreed before production is initiated. Instead, the risk that banks bear is the credit risk, because the reimbursement of credits is never guaranteed.

By using accounting methods, we can clarify the creation of money by the commercial banks. We shall use a quite simple example to illustrate this, ignoring all banking business apart from granting credits and assuming that all payments are made in bank money, that is, by deposit transactions, central bank money therefore

[3] Josef Ackermann describes cash holding by banks in detail as follows: It "consists of central bank money, hence of cash and on demand credit balances at central banks. If for the time being we consider only the connections between credit institutes and the non-banking sector, changes in the cash balance arise from the demand for notes and the supply of notes by the banks arising from their deposit and credit activity. A credit bank needs central bank money so that it can make payments related to the activity on its asset and liability accounts. Such payments have to be made to creditors of the bank who want central bank money, or to borrowers who wish to make a withdrawal in notes on the credit they possess. They also have to be made to other credit institutions in the course of transactions arising if customers make a transfer to an agent who has an account at another bank. . . . Since it is usually the case that payments in and out of a bank in central bank money over any one period generally coincide, the bank only needs to hold a relatively small amount of central bank money to secure its liquidity. . . . Credit institutions can therefore reduce their cash balances in relation to turnover to a far greater degree than firms can. They can not only for the most part constantly balance the demand for and supply of notes in their transactions with the non-banking sector; they are also able to iron out peaks in payments among themselves through the clearing system. In addition to this a credit institution can purchase central bank money. If for example the prevailing level of cash holdings is smaller than the desired and necessary balance, central bank money is demanded by the banks and offer in exchange secondary liquid assets. Such secondary liquid assets are especially money market paper, rediscountable bills and securities. The actual level of cash held becomes a balance resulting from transactions with the non-banking sector, reduced by excess supply or increased by excess demand of central bank money in the money market" (Ackermann 1977, 112f.).

being needed only as a legal minimum requirement. All deposits are sight deposits, hence bank money. The only costs that fall to the bank are the payment of wages.

The *bank* is here representative of all banks, so that sight deposits can be a multiple of the central bank money which the bank has to hold to meet reserve requirements. In our example the scope for the extension of further credit has not yet been exhausted, so that in the year we consider further credit can be extended.

The *bank* starts with an equity capital of 100 money units and sight deposits of 200 money units. We envisage the following scenario preceding our starting point: Through the issuing of bank notes, the central bank has received 300 money units of coin from nonbanks. The nonbanks buy for 100 units of bank notes' shares of the *bank,* which becomes the bank's equity, and exchange 200 money units against sight deposits with the *bank*. The *bank* hands over 300 money units to the central bank and receives in return a corresponding credit with the central bank.

There is a requirement to hold a minimum reserve of 33 %. This means that the *bank* can advance credits (loans) in the form of sight deposits to the amount of 700 money units, without infringing the minimum requirement. With this, the sight deposits credited to the *bank* at the central bank become 900 money units, 300 units being the minimum reserve (300 = 1/3 × 900 money units). This represents the maximum of the creation of credit and money at a given central bank credit for the *bank*, given the regulation on minimum reserves.

We further assume that the rate of interest for bank credit is 5 %. This means that the credit user has to pay an annual interest of 35 money units (5 % × 700 money units = 35 money units). Payment is made by a corresponding reduction of the sight deposits of the borrowers. Salaries are paid by crediting sight deposits. We assume that these amount to 20 money units.

The balance sheet of the *bank* is therefore:

BALANCE SHEET

Assets		Liabilities & Stockholders' Equity	
Credit balance with Central bank	300	Sight desposits (Bank Money)	200
		Equity capital	100
Total	300	Total	300

The entries resulting from credit granting, salary expense, and interest payments are:

	Debit	Credit
a. Credit	700	
Sight deposit		700
b. Salary expense	20	
Sight deposit		20
c. Sight deposit	35	
Interest		35

ASSETS
Credits

a.	700		
Balance	700		

LIABILITIES
Sight deposit

		Balance	200
		a.	700
c.	35	b.	20
		Balance	885

REVENUES
Interest

		c.	35
		Balance	35

EXPENSES
Salary expense

b.	20		
Balance	20		

The closing entries in the income summary are:

	Debit	Credit
d. Income summary	20	
Salary expense		20
e. Interest	35	
Income summary		35

Income summary

d.	20	e.	35
Net profit	15		
		Balance	0

REVENUES
Interest

e.	35	c.	35
Balance	0		

EXPENSES
Salary expense

b.	20	d.	20
		Balance	0

The outcome is that with equity capital of 100 and a net profit of 15, the return on equity is 15 %.

We assume that two-thirds of the profit is paid out as dividends and that one-third is added to equity capital. The related entries are:

	Debit	Credit
f. Income summary	15	
Distribution of profits		15
g. Distribution of profits	5	
Equity capital		5
h. Distribution of profits	10	
Sight deposits		10

Distribution of profits			
g.	5	f.	15
h.	10		
		Balance	0

LIABILITIES Sight deposit			
c.	35	Balance	200
		a.	700
		b.	20
		h.	10
		Balance	895

STOCKHOLDERS' EQUITY Equity capital			
		Balance	100
		g.	5
		Balance	105

Correspondingly, the balance sheet at the end of the year looks as follows:

BALANCE SHEET

Assets		Liabilities & Stockholders' Equity	
Credit balance with Central bank	300	Sight desposit (Bank money)	895
Credit (bank customer)	700	Equity capital	105
Total	1000	Total	1000

In this example, profit arises from the difference between the interest which borrowers pay for their credit and the costs of banking activity. Interest payments are made by the reduction of the borrowers' sight deposits, thus by a reduction of bank debt. The sight deposits move back up again as far as the profit is paid out as dividend. The bank's equity capital is increased by any retained profits, and since sight deposits are money, but equity capital is not, the amount of money is reduced. Bank money is partially covered by central bank money but primarily through the credits which the bank has extended in the form of bank money. In this sense, the creation of credit and money is a self-referential process which in principle—taking account of the possibilities of refinancing through the central bank—can proceed to infinity. Since credit is either rolled over or new credit replaces the old, the quantity of money simply grows from period to period in the historical process.

If banks benefit from the absence of the market risk to which commodity production is exposed, they are however confronted with a high level of credit risk, as previously noted. This chiefly affects their main business, the extension of credit to firms. Credit risk arises from the fact that firms have to pay interest for the duration of the credit and then have to repay the principal, or at any rate be in a position to repay the principal, although they no longer have the money which they originally gained by raising credit. Credit was raised to make investments and to increase the production. The firm is only able to pay interest and repay the principal if it has in the meantime achieved a surplus of revenue over costs, in other words, made a profit from which they can pay interest. This can normally be taken for granted, since it is in the firm's interest to raise credit and begin and enlarge the production only if they calculate that they will make a profit. But it is always possible that market risk has been miscalculated and that there are losses instead of profits. This circumstance compels the banks to protect themselves against this risk to the credit they grant, and they generally do this by granting credit only to those firms that have sufficient equity capital. In addition to this, the credit is secured by collateral. This presupposes that the borrowing firm possesses real property, especially land and buildings. Real property therefore serves—as Gunnar Heinsohn and Otto Steiger (1996) have shown—also as the necessary condition of the production of money it is used to secure credits.

Banks also insure themselves by granting credit not only to private persons and institutions but also to the government—mostly through the purchase of treasury bonds or government debt on the open market. Government debts deemed as being secure, since by definition the state cannot go bankrupt at least in terms of its own currency. The reality behind government debt is the power of the state. If necessary, it can raise new taxes as well as compel the central bank, which was itself created by the state, to provide it with credit as an emergency measure. The central bank is able to do this at any time, since its money can no longer be redeemed with gold. The state is therefore always able to honor its debt at least if its currency represents a leading currency. George Shackle commented on this that "the practical necessities of life drive us to accept some things as unquestionable: sunrise and sunset, eventual personal dissolution and the payment of due interest by the British Government." (Shackle 1968, p. 141)

4.2 Interest in the Modern Monetary Economy: Interest as the Price of Credit

If we take into account what interest actually means in practice, the phenomenon of interest can be explained very easily. It is simply the price of credit. Why can lender of money charge a price for the credit? For no other reason, he owns the good which he is lending. In our legal order, any owner of a good has the right, irrespective if whether he inherited, purchased, or produced it, to charge a price for handing over his good, even if this is only temporary.

The level of this price was originally determined by the amount of savings. This amount was relatively small with regard to the demand, and therefore, the interest level comparatively high. Since today money consists mainly of bank money that is produced by bank granting credits and that for this reason the amount of credits can increase far beyond the amount of savings, the interest level is much lower as it was before. Its level has at the minimum to cover the production costs of bank money. These costs are first of all the costs of running the banks themselves, secondly the interests to be paid on saving deposits, and thirdly the refinancing costs when the banks need central bank money. Above and beyond these costs, the banks can set a profit margin as compensation for their exposure to risk and as an additional surplus. This additional surplus arises from the simple fact that all banks enjoy *together* a legal monopoly of the creation of money by granting credits.

Fig. 4.1 The growth of the quantity of money on the basis of the rate of interest set by the Central Bank

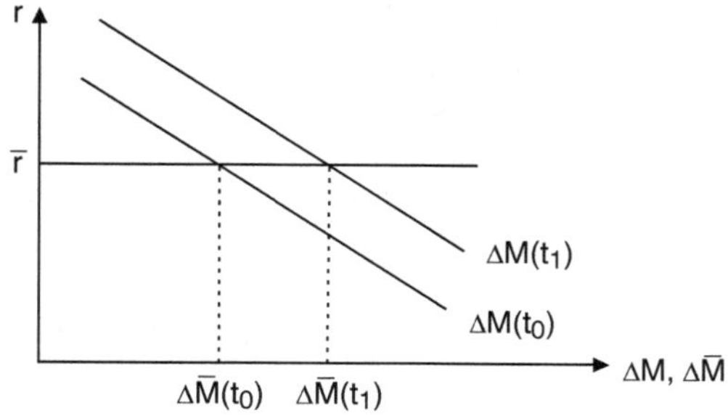

Shortly after the First World War, L. A. Hahn argued that

> today the extension of credit based upon saved money is the exception, while the granting of credit through the *ad hoc* creation of bank purchasing power the rule. In principle person B can be rendered capable of purchasing even if person A has saved nothing, but has spent all the proceeds of his product himself. (Hahn 1920, p. 117)

According to this quote, it has to be realized that banks can grant credits even when nobody saves or dishoards money, and bank customers hold only sight deposits as money.[4] Saving in the form of saving deposits at a bank plays a secondary role, being of significance only to the extent that for saving deposits the banks have to hold less central bank money if sight deposits are transformed into saving deposits and so can reduce the refinancing requirement.

This does not mean that no savings are required to finance investments. They are in fact an important precondition. But this is primarily related to the building of equity capital. Apart from start-up financing, this mainly consists of savings built up by the firm through retained profits.

The support given by the central bank to the creation of money leads to a determination of the price in the credit and money market in a quite different way as the determination of the price in the market of commodities. In this market supply and demand determine the price of the commodity. In the credit and money market, the reverse occurs. Here the demand determines together with the fixed price—the rate of interest—the supply of money. The main condition is that the borrower has sufficient equity capital to provide security to the creditor. If we assume that this is the case, the money and credit market can be represented graphically in terms of the conventional framework of supply and demand. If we ignore the distinction between short- and long-term interest rates, we can represent the growth of the quantity of money and credit $\Delta\bar{M}(t)$ as the intercept of a downward-sloping demand curve $\Delta M(t)$ for new credit, that is, for additional

[4] This does not prevent the creation of money being treated as ex post savings in national income accounts, since all income that is not consumed is treated as "saving," and in a closed economy investment is always equated ex post with savings, so that ex post the equation $I = S$ can be assumed.

money, and the horizontal supply curve given by the rate of interest $\bar{r}$ set mainly by the refinancing conditions of the central bank (See Fig. 4.1).

The demand rises inversely to the rate of interest since more investment projects become profitable and more credit will be demanded the lower the rate of interest. At a given rate of interest, the demand for credit or money will be the higher—the demand curve will be located further to the right—the longer the period for which credit is needed. We should also bear in mind that new investment projects are constantly emerging. So the demand for credit will be renewed and enlarged from period to period.

The central bank will seek to adapt to the given situation. On the one hand, the rate of interest should keep money sufficiently scarce in order to avoid excessive inflation. On the other hand, the rate of interest should be sufficiently low, such that the demand for credit persists, that is, the rate of interest should be below the average rate of profit.

Part II

Market and Production

5 The Development of the Theories of Production: Valid Insights and Shortcomings

5.1 Overview of the Theories of Production

In part one we examined the relationship between market and money. Our next step is to consider the *theory of production* in more details, for explaining how production and the market interact with each other, with production following the dynamics of the market.

In considering *this interaction*, we discover that there are two basic approaches, each with completely different perspectives. The first approach is the *net product theory or surplus theory*, which primarily addresses the issues of the continued creation of wealth. The second is the *marginal productivity theory*, which assumes that all important resources are in short supply and therefore focuses on the optimal use of those limited resources. The *net product theory* is the theory of the physiocrats in the eighteenth century, the theory of the mercantilists in the seventeenth and eighteenth centuries, and the theory of the classical economists in the late eighteenth and in the nineteenth centuries. The physiocrats considered land (nature) as the major source of wealth, while the mercantilists and the classical economists focused on labor as the major source of wealth. The *marginal productivity theory* is the theory of the neoclassical economists of the nineteenth century. The conventional theory of production as taught today in contemporary microeconomic textbooks is based on the latter.

All theories of production have led to valid insights. But each of them also has its shortcomings. The challenge is to overcome the deficiencies and bring the valid insights into a logical context. At the same time, one should constantly bear in mind that all of these theories are rooted in the specific historical and institutional settings of their time. It is the merit of the historical school of economics and their followers that these presuppositions were made explicit and that they pointed out the significance of economic development over time together with the corresponding institutional or technical changes. For that reason, we will also address these approaches.

In all theories of production, the question of how the social product is distributed is also of great interest. For that reason, theories of production and theories of

H.C. Binswanger, *The Growth Spiral*, DOI 10.1007/978-3-642-31881-8_5,

distribution should always be considered together, with the theory of production being a prerequisite for the theory of distribution. One can even say that the differences between the theories of production are largely attributable to the differing views on the (correct) distribution of the social product.

5.2 The Net Product Theory of the Physiocratic School Based on the Value Theory of Land – Supplemented by a Value Theory of Imagination

The productivity of land is central to the physiocratic theory. Physiocracy developed in eighteenth-century France. Its most significant representatives are François Quesnay (1679–1774) and Anne Robert Jacques Turgot (1727–1781). Both authors assume that a portion of the agricultural yield would be necessary for the subsistence, that is, the living expenses of the farmer and his family, as well as for maintaining the farm and for providing the seed necessary for growing crops the following year. All these expenses are termed *reprises* by the physiocrats. They will be called "restitution costs" in this book. The difference between the total product and the restitution costs is the net product (*produit net*) or the surplus. The essential factor for the physiocrats was the fact that land requires no restitution costs. The services of the land cost nothing because the productivity of the land is constantly restored as part of the ecological cycle, with support from the sun's energy without additional costs. Therefore, 100 % of the land's—or nature's—contribution to the production belongs to the surplus or net product. Turgot describes the contribution of land in the creation of surplus more as a physical consequence of the fertility of the soil than of the amount of effort and skill the farmer has employed to render the soil fertile. Turgot argues that the soil, independent of any agreement, pays the farmer immediately the price of his toil. Nature does not bargain with the farmer or force him to be satisfied with just the absolute necessities. The farmer, besides his subsistence, harvests products which he has not purchased, but which he can sell (see Turgot 1981, 99f.).

It is assumed in this statement that the farmer receives not only that portion of the income he or his family requires for subsistence but also the net product or the surplus. However, this is only valid in theory and not in the historical context of France in eighteenth century, where the farmer's net product had to be paid to the landlords as a rent. This historical context corresponds to the standard physiocratic representation of economic flow. But a third solution for the allocation of the net product may also be possible, an allocation neither to the farmer nor to the landlord but to the consumer. This would be the case if the farmer himself is the owner of the land and therefore must not pay any rent to a landlord, but thanks to the competition of the farmers, the prices of agricultural products are forced down to the level of restitution costs. In this case we have a consumer rent instead of a rent paid to the landlords. The net product is not lost; it just does not appear in form of a monetary income. However, the actual result—the creation of net product—remains the same.

The physiocrats developed the net product theory with a model in which the surplus of a given year's harvest is fully consumed, so that nothing remains for net investments. But the model was not meant as a description of actual conditions, that is, of conditions in eighteenth-century France, but rather as a state to be strived for. In order to achieve this state, the landowners were supposed—and this was an essential physiocratic postulate—to reinvest a portion of the surplus paid to them as rent in order to increase the annual yield, which was exceedingly low at the time.

The portion of the total production that the farmers require as restitution costs Quesnay refers to as the landowners' advances (*avances*) to the farmers. The landowners grant advances to ensure that they will receive their rent again in the following year. This involves, on the one hand, the annual advances (*avances annuelles*) or circulating capital. This is the portion of the revenues that is to be used to maintain the farm, which recurs every single year, that is, the portion of the revenues that provide for the farmers' living and the provision of seed, etc. On the other hand, there is also the primitive advances (*avances primitives*) or fixed capital that is to be used for reinvesting in the farm, such as the restoration or repair of buildings and implements. The term "advances" is used because the time sequence of planting and harvest must be taken into account. Its consideration serves to provide a more precise chronological structure of the production process. From the time of sowing on, one must live on the previous year's harvest (see Quesnay 1924).

The physiocrats did not claim that the land alone produces the surplus, but for them labor can be productive only if it works together with nature.[1] According to their opinion, labor, which merely transforms the raw materials, produces no surplus and is, therefore, "sterile." This refers to the labor in manufacturing. This point of view does not recognize the productive service of manufacturing workers, who process a few initial products into hundreds of different finished products, thereby immensely increasing the value of the initial products. This is only possible thanks to human imagination, which continually conceives new products and thus also creates a surplus, if not in quantity then in value.

By recognizing the value creation in manufacturing, the German economist Johann Georg Schlosser (1739–1799) extends the physiocratic theory in this respect.[2] He acknowledges that a surplus was created through the manufacture of final products, which he terms "forms." They satisfy "imaginary" wants that exist latently but are actually revealed only in the moment the products concerned are produced and supplied to the market. In this way he supplements the French value theory of land with a—as we like to call it—value theory of imagination.

Schlosser clarifies the meaning of "forms" by illustrating them with an example from ancient Athens. He states:

[1] cf. Birger P. Priddat (2002, p. 67): "The travail productif defined here is not based on a reshaping of materials from nature but rather on a stimulation of the potential hidden in nature."

[2] cf. Rainer Klump (2000), Birger P. Priddat (2000), and Hans Ch. Binswanger (2000).

> Calculate . . . what an astounding mass of manpower . . . in the single city of Athens is put in motion in order to satisfy [imaginary] wants, and how this relates to the mass of material consumed in this same town. Surely, [one will] find that the relationship is as 1 to 100. Take just one single statue by Praxiteles and calculate what he expended in artistic effort, time, diligence, and manpower on it and how this effort relates to the ore out of which he made the statue and to the expense of feeding him while he worked. (Schlosser 2000, p. 70)

Schlosser notes that the surplus produced by the manufacturing is, as a rule, even substantially higher than in the agricultural sector, not despite but because the former is less close to nature and, thus, is also capable of serving rather artificial, increasingly sophisticated wants. To a great extent, these wants emanate from a boundless human fantasy and therefore can, in principle, never be satisfied.

Nevertheless, Schlosser accepts the physiocratic model with its concept of surplus. So in this sense, he remains a physiocrat. He just says: "The class of artists, manufacturers and merchants is not non-productive; they produce imaginary commodities for imaginary wants" (Schlosser 1777, p. 43). He is actually saying here that nonagricultural labor also produces surplus. This assessment is equally, or even more, valid for the industry that, since the industrial revolution, has been producing not only hundreds but thousands upon thousands of different commodities, all with the intention of creating new wants, of expanding the value horizon. This point ought to be kept in mind when the inclusion of nature is discussed in the following pages. It is always about the inclusion of nature *with* its transformations by human imagination.

5.3 The Net Product Theory of the Mercantilist and the Classical Economic Doctrines Based on the Value Theory of Labor

The physiocratic value theory of land was replaced by the classical value theory of labor, developed in Great Britain in the eighteenth/nineteenth century, for which the groundwork had been laid already by the mercantilists in the seventeenth century. The classical value theory of labor disregards the contribution of the soil; only labor is seen to be productive. But the theory was also focused on the net product, which is income not committed to restitution expenses. Classical economists assumed, as did the physiocrats and the mercantilists before them, that solely labor requires restitution expenses. Thus, the worker—whether in agriculture, in trade, or in industry—is allotted an income only sufficient to make his "restitution" possible, that is, a subsistence wage. However, in contrast to the physiocrats, it was not simply the issue of achieving a surplus what concerned them most but rather the continuous increase of the surplus, which they primarily ascribed to the division of labor and a constant expansion of production. The division of labor implies that an advance must be provided in form of a wage fund as well as a fund for the purchase of means of production in order to concentrate the workers in agricultural enterprises (large farms) or industrial companies (factories) on suitable sites, thereby rendering possible a specialization of workers in specific activities. This advance is the firm's capital. Without capital to invest, there is no business. For that reason, the term "advance" has a totally different meaning for the classical economists than it does for the physiocrats. The physiocrats were primarily concerned with the sequential chronology of production and consumption resulting from the natural order of sowing followed by harvesting. In contrast to that, firm's capital is an advance that must be provided deliberately to start an enterprise. As every advance is risky, a compensation has to be paid in the form of a profit. The profit is part of the surplus.

Adam Smith, and all the classical economists along with him, did therefore not consider capital to be a factor of production but a factor which increases and promotes labor's productivity. For classical economists capital therefore is rather to be called a factor of promotion (see above p. 15).[3] Assigning the surplus to capital in the form of profit was in marked contrast to the theory of the physiocrats, who allocated the surplus to the land in the form of a land rent due to the productivity of the land. In order to reserve the surplus for the profit of capital, the classical economists divested land of its status as a factor of production. As a consequence, the landowners were able to claim a share of the surplus only due to property rights but no longer because of the land's own productive contribution.

Mercantilists had already laid the groundwork for the classical value theory of labor by considering land's contribution to the national product as being practically insignificant, although they did not eliminate it all together. The theories of William Petty (1623–1687) and John Locke (1632–1704), who respectively had the Irish and English conditions in mind, were decisive in this regard.

Petty (1691) addressed the issue of the productive contributions of land and labor by comparing the income from a particular piece of uncultivated land with the income from a piece of cultivated land. He only credited the land with the income from the uncultivated land, while he credited labor with all of the surplus from the cultivated land, which was, of course, many times more than the income from the uncultivated land.[4,5]

---

[3] The concept of capital as an advance can already be found in a statement of Turgot: The owner of capital will employ his "advance[s] partly for the construction of the establishment and the purchase of materials, partly for the daily wages of the workmen ... " (Turgot 1981, p. 137). The profit is earned for the use of the money as an advance, with the compensation for the risk that the businessman takes along with the reward for his business acumen playing an essential role. Turgot says that "with money we can furnish means for cultivation, establish manufactures, and set up trade. The profits of which accumulated and frugally saved, will become a new capital; since in short, money is the principal means of begetting money" (Turgot 1981, p. 147). To this extent, Turgot was even more modern than the classical economists, who perceived the relationship between money and profit, but did not include it in their theory.

[4] It is important to keep in mind that Petty, who worked in Ireland, based his observations on the situation there of extensive farming where the cattle could pasture day and night in open fields in summer and winter, and the cultivation and care of the land was not necessary.

[5] Petty's concept of the net product theory is explained in detail by Tony Aspromourgos (2005).

John Locke adopted Petty's argumentation and took it to the extreme with the following statement:

> Nor is it so strange, as perhaps before consideration it may appear, that the property of labour should be able to over-balance the community of land: for it is labour indeed that puts the difference of value on every thing; and let any one consider what the difference is between an acre of land planted with tobacco or sugar, sown with wheat or barley, and an acre of the same land lying in common, without any husbandry upon it, and he will find, that the improvement of labor makes the far greater part of the value. I think it will be but a very modest computation to say that of the products of the earth useful to the life of man nine tenths are the effects of labor; nay, if we will rightly estimate things as they come to our use, and cast up the several expenses about them—what in them is purely owing to nature, and what to labour—we shall find, that in most of them ninety-nine hundredths are wholly to be put on the account of labour. (John Locke 1946, 21f.)

Yet land and labor cooperate with each other. The disregard of this obvious fact by the mercantilists can be traced to their view that the land was, so to speak, a "conservative" and labor was a "progressive" factor, since laborers were not only employed to till the land but also to improve its productivity and to process its products. Significantly more than the physiocrats of eighteenth-century France, the mercantilists considered themselves to be representatives of "progress," that is, of an economy that was constantly further developing.

This dynamic of progress also became decisive for the English classical economists, although the two main proponents of classical economy, Adam Smith and David Ricardo (1772–1823), reasoned differently. After all, Adam Smith was still speaking of an annual national product as being a "labor *and* land product." This would explain why he occasionally recognizes a productive contribution of land and, in doing so, renders the physiocratic doctrine a certain reverence. En passant he even justifies ground rent with the productive contribution of land or nature in a physiocratic manner in a passage in his *Wealth of Nations*. He writes:

> This rent may be considered as the produce of those powers of nature, the use of which the landlord lends to the farmer. It is greater or smaller according to the supposed extent of those powers, or in other words, according to the supposed natural or improved fertility of the land. It is the work of nature which remains after deducting or compensating everything which can be regarded as the work of man. It is seldom less than a fourth, and frequently more than a third of the whole produce. (Smith 1976, Bk II, Ch V, 385)

In this statement Adam Smith assesses nature's contribution to be significantly higher than did the mercantilists, without any particular justification.

However, in the main, Adam Smith holds tight to the thesis that the wealth of nations is created solely by labor, proclaiming with great emphasis at the beginning of his book: "Labor was the first price, the original purchase-money that was paid for all things" (Smith 1976, Bk I, Ch V, 35). Accordingly, the landowner is reduced to a parasite: "As soon as the land of any country has all become private property, the landlords, like all other men, love to reap where they never sowed, and demand a rent even for its natural produce" (Smith 1976, Bk I, Ch VI, 56).

In order to avoid the discrepancies between the land theory of value and the labor theory of value, Smith employs a version of the labor theory of value that makes labor alone the measure of a product's *relative* value. It becomes, as he terms it, "the real value of all the different component parts of price ... measured by the quantity of labor which they can, each of them, purchase or command. Labor measures the value not only of that part of price which resolves itself into labor, but of that which resolves itself into rent, and of that which resolves itself into profit" (Smith 1976, Bk I, Ch VI, 56). What counts then is only labor, and the exchange value or price is determined by the amount of labor.

David Ricardo is essentially a more radical representative of the labor theory of value. For him, work is the only production factor because it is the only factor that generates restitution costs, the mandatory price of labor paid in wages. It must be paid to retain the laborer as a production factor. This does not hold true for land because it regenerates or restores itself.

Unlike Adam Smith, Ricardo does not make the assumption that all land had been divided up as private property because he considers the possibility of including agricultural imports from America, where in his days new land was constantly being cultivated without the necessity of paying a ground rent for that new land. The land was for the immigrants a free commodity. Whoever took possession of the land became its owner. Here Ricardo supposes that the better land with the higher fertility will always be appropriated and cultivated first so that the yield of any new and therefore less fertile land—he speaks of marginal land—is always the lowest. The owner of the fertile land—and he alone—could therefore demand a rent from a possible tenant corresponding to the difference between the yield of the fertile land he appropriated and the yield of the marginal land. Even though he speaks of the "original and indestructible powers of the soil" (Ricardo 1951, p. 67) that is crucial to production, Ricardo considers land not to be a factor of production, because a ground rent is not paid for all land but only for a portion of it.

The difference between Adam Smith's theory of rent that allows a rent for all land and Ricardo's differential rent theory is nevertheless smaller than it appears at first glance. It is a simple consequence of Adam Smith assuming that all land is owned and therefore scarce and so the rent is to be regarded as a collective monopoly, while Ricardo considers only fertile land to be scarce so that the owners of this fertile land possess only a partial monopoly to the extent of the fertility of their land. Either way, ground rents appear in the classical theory essentially as a deduction from the earnings of labor, which is only justified by the property laws, in relationship to the respective scarcity of land. Despite the occasional recognition of the productive powers of land or nature, both Smith and Ricardo place the distribution aspect before the production aspect, thus putting a magic hood of invisibility over nature, condemning it to remain unseen, although its production powers are of course always at work.

When the classical economists more or less striped land of its status as a factor of production—as Adam Smith does with reservations and Ricardo more radically—it is all the more astonishing that they did not recognize the new contribution nature makes to the development of industry, namely, as mechanical energy, which was and is the foundation of the industrial revolution and of economic growth.

The assumption could be made that at least Adam Smith may be excused for not emphasizing the significance of energy because coal-driven steam engines were not in use in his days. This assumption, however, is inaccurate. Although 1776, the year that *The Wealth of Nations* was published, is often mentioned as the date of James Watt's invention of the steam engine, it was a much longer process. There were several preliminary designs leading to the machine of 1776 that were apparently known to Adam Smith. He alluded more than once to the importance of the "powers in nature" in an early draft of *The Wealth of Nations* (see Weismahr 1992, 69f). He also specifically speaks of "fire engines" using "a power in nature which had never before been thought of" (Adam Smith, *Glasgow Edition of the Works and Correspondence* Vol. 5, Lectures On Jurisprudence, Chap. 2). "Power in nature" was an early term for energy. But all passages relating to energy were discarded by Smith in his final version of *The Wealth of Nations* (1776). He did only leave a few references to machines. But how are machines to be run without energy?

In the final version of *The Wealth of Nations*, Smith even goes so far as to claim that although nature has a hand in agriculture, it does not in industry, and in fact states: "In them nature does nothing; man does all" (Smith 1976, Bk II, Ch V, p. 385). At least David Ricardo appeared surprised at this statement. In a footnote in his *Principles* (1817)—in the chapter on rents—he asks: "Does nature nothing for man in manufactures? Are the powers of wind and water, which move our machinery, and assist navigation, nothing? The pressure of the atmosphere and the elasticity of steam, which enable us to work the most stupendous engines—are they not the gifts of nature? To say nothing of the effects of the matter of heat in softening and melting metals, of the decomposition of the atmosphere in the process of dyeing and fermentation" (Ricardo 1951, p. 76, see also Weismahr 1992, 70f). But Ricardo also does not further mention the immanent power of nature (energy) outside of this footnote, although the steam engine was already widely in use in his days.

John Stuart Mill, the last of the major representatives of English classical economists, at least sees power in nature as an independent production factor that can take the place of labor. He writes in his *Principles of Political Economy*: "The requisites of production are two: labor, and appropriate natural objects. . . . Nature, however, does more than supply materials; she also supplies powers. The matter of the globe is not an inert recipient of forms and properties impressed by human hands; it has active energies by which it co-operates with, and may even be used as a substitute for labor[!]" (Mill 1899, Vol. I, 45f.). But Mill, as well, did not take this insight into account in the rest of his deliberations.

The omission of the powers in nature/energy is particularly disturbing when Adam Smith explains the advantages of specialization in consequence of the division of labor. These advantages, he argues, are owned to three different circumstances: first, "to the increase of dexterity in every particular workman" that can be gained through the workman specializing in certain tasks; secondly, "to the saving of the time which is commonly lost in passing from one species of work to another"; and thirdly, "to the invention of a great number of machines which facilitate and abridge labor, and enable one man to do the work of many" (Smith, 1976, Bk I, Ch I, p. 11).

The perception, which is generally accepted still today, is that the advantages of specialization and the resulting increase in productivity as portrayed by Smith could simply result in the course of time—and only in the course of time—because dexterity increases with time and, thanks to organizational progress, the time lost by changing workplaces is constantly decreasing. This increase in productivity could also be seen as an increase in the number of a virtual labor force, given that they make one worker capable of doing the work of many. But, when Adam Smith speaks of machines, he never mentions that they run on steam and that this steam is produced by heating water with burning coal. Thus, the advantages of specialization and division of work remain a phenomenon that seems to concern labor alone.

However, the great advances in production that mark the industrial revolution did of course result from the introduction of energy, the use of which greatly increased the productivity of labor in connection with the specialization and the division of labor. This means that nature—land or natural resources, which supplies also the energy-is not only a value creator in agriculture but in industry as well. In both, nature must be acknowledged as an independent factor of production.

If nature was no longer considered to be a creator of value, more or less elevating labor to be the one and only production factor, it did not imply—as we have already pointed out—that the workers should be granted all of the income realized from the production. On this point, the physiocrats, mercantilists, and classic economists were all in agreement. Up until the beginning of the nineteenth century, it was almost taken for granted that the workers in both agriculture and industry would earn only subsistence wages, meaning wages equivalent to the restitution costs of labor. The surplus or net product, according to the classical economists, belongs only to the owners of capital and of land—to the owners of capital because of the role of capital as a factor of promotion and to the owners of land because of their property rights.

The competition for jobs among the workers was apparently fiercer than the sales competition among the firms, so that the workers' wages could be reduced to a greater extent than the commodity prices. Adam Smith was the only one to concede that the demand for labor during economic growth could increase faster than the supply of labor, so that wages could rise above the subsistence level. But such an increase was hardly discernable in the early nineteenth century.

The classical labor theory of value, notably in its Ricardian form, could easily be interpreted as a theory of exploitation. If nature was no longer recognized as a factor of production, and—this in contrast to the classical theory—the role of capital as a factor of promotion was ignored, labor was left as the only value-creating factor, so that both rents and profits must appear as deductions from the earnings that labor deserves, in other words, as exploitation. This resulted in the demand that workers be given all the earnings—a demand raised both by the Ricardian socialists in England, such as Thomas Hodgskin (1787–1869) and John Bray (1809–1897), the French socialists, above all by Pierre Joseph Proudhon (1809–1865), and the

German socialists; of them, it was Karl Marx (1818–1883), who delivered the most detailed justification.[6]

Marx argued that a worker who labored 12 hours produces a product with a value of 12 hours, but if the equivalent of 6 hours of labor was enough to ensure subsistence for him and his family, he only receives that equivalent as wage. Solely by virtue of the fact that the capitalist, as the owner of the capital, has a claim to the income from the sale of the product, he can deprive the worker of the added value of 6 hours of his labor, in other words, exploit him. When Adam Smith says of the landlords that they "love to reap where they never sowed," Karl Marx added that capitalists earn where they have never worked.

In this way, Marx brushes aside the role that capital plays as a factor of promotion, even though he occasionally admits it.[7]

Excursus

The Elimination of Money in the Classical Theory as a Consequence of the Dispute with Mercantilism

Why was the identification of capital as an advance neglected by the followers of classical economists, despite Adam Smith having explicitly emphasized it? Our hypothesis is that it had to do with the failure of the classical economists to recognize the significance of money in building capital even though—or maybe because—it was so strongly stressed by their predecessors, the mercantilists.

The classical economists were in opposition to mercantilism despite the fact that they had adopted their labor value theory. The bone of contention for the classical economists opposed the protectionist trade policies demanded by the mercantilists in England and France. The purpose of mercantile protectionism was to bring about an influx of gold and silver from Spain and Portugal in order to increase the money supply and, with it, the stock of capital in their own countries. More specifically, they proposed import barriers for manufactured goods *from* Spain and Portugal and support for the export of manufactured goods *to* these countries with the goal to achieve a trade surplus in trading with these countries, that is, force a trade deficit upon them which they in turn were to pay for in gold or silver. In this way France and England wanted to profit from the influx of gold and silver from Central and South America going to the Iberian Peninsula.

(continued)

[6] See Hodgskin (1964), Bray (1957), Proudhon (1847/1849), Marx/Engels (1956).

[7] In a dispute with Adolf Wagner, Marx wrote: "At any rate, in my presentation even, profit on capital is in actual fact not only a subtraction from, or a robbery of the worker. On the contrary, I depict the capitalist as the necessary functionary of capitalist production and demonstrate at great length that he not only subtracts or 'robs' but enforces the production of surplus value, thus first helping to create what is to be subtracted" (Karl Marx, Notes on A. Wagner, in: Marx/Engels 1956, vol. 19, p. 358). This quotation makes clear that the classical understanding of the capital as a factor of promotion also had its influence on Marx, though only marginally. The theory of exploitation takes center place with him. See Hans G. Nutzinger (1974, 68f.).

Contrary to the mercantilists, the classical economists demanded an unconditional free trade policy—much in line with the physiocrats in this respect—including the elimination of all national trade barriers and of trade promotion. To achieve this goal, they had to question the justification of a gold and silver money influx. They did thus reject protectionist trade policies with the claim that an inflow of gold and silver would not lead to any advantage for their countries, since the increase of the amount of money would only induce an increase in prices and did thus have no real impact.[8] They based their arguments on the so-called quantity theory of money which does not address the relation between money influx and the formation of capital.

Consequently, they dismissed the possibility of considering John Locke's argument that the gold and silver inflow from Central and South America to Spain and Portugal had led to lower interest rates with an accompanying increase in investments. According to Locke, the inflow of gold and silver would have the same effect in England if the gold and silver inflow could be redirected there. But referring to David Hume (1711–1776), Adam Smith believed he could disprove Locke's argument by assuming an increase in the price level proportional to the inflow of money, with the result that the purchasing power of both, capital and interest, decreased by the same proportion so that the relation between the two, that is, the rate of interest, remained constant (see Smith 1976, Bk II, Ch IV, p. 377). He did not see that, as Locke assumed, a portion of the money influx arrives *first* in the credit market *before* it will be spent on purchasing goods; with the increasing money supply, the interest rate decreases, resulting in an increase of investments. Consequently, the quantity theory of money did not, or only to a limited extent, apply.[9]

Nevertheless, it should be noted that in Adam Smith's time paper money was already playing a certain role. His arguments in this respect are more refined. He admits that the substitution of gold and silver with paper money saves manpower that would otherwise need to go into the production of gold and silver. The manpower saved could be used elsewhere so that the actual social product could increase due to paper money production. But Adam Smith thought that any increase in the supply of paper money *beyond* the corresponding savings in manpower for the production of gold and silver would equally lead to rising prices, just as would an increase in the gold and silver supply.

(continued)

[8] See also Erich Streissler (1999b, p. 27): With his claim that the supply of money only influences prices, Adam Smith explicitly stresses "that with this statement he is targeting a certain system of the political economy, specifically mercantilism."

[9] The mercantilists' understanding of the production-promoting effect of increasing the money supply is also underscored by Karl-Heinz Schmidt (1994, p. 40): "The increase in the money supply is meant to contribute to the creation of new jobs in trade and industry, to make one's own country independent from the import of important industrial goods, and by doing so to expand the nation's economic and political power."

Smith did thus disregard the reasoning for issuing paper money formulated by John Law (1671–1729), a later mercantilist. In his text, *Money and Trade Considered with a Proposal for Supplying the Nation with Money*, Law pointed out that, while increasing the supply of gold and silver money could lead to price increases, increasing the supply of paper money would not. This is because paper money goes into circulation through bank loans used to fund investments and does thus lead to a corresponding increase in production. In this way, an increase in the supply of paper money does automatically lead to an increase in the real social product, so that no or only minor price increases occur.[10] Law's reasoning culminates in the statement that "An addition to the money adds to the value of the country" (Law 1934, p. 158).

But John Law did not sufficiently take into account that an increase in the money supply can also occur via public debt without a corresponding increase in production, nor did he sufficiently consider the possibility of speculative bubbles. On the other hand, Adam Smith did only pay marginal attention to the issuance of paper money via investment financing and the related increase in production, even though the increase in money supply via the issuance of paper money was possible without protectionist trade policy, that is, there was no longer a contradiction with the classical postulate of free trade. Assuming a roughly equal increase in money supply in all countries participating in international trade, national paper money printing did not only go well with free trade but was even a precondition for the trade expansion following increased investments. But Adam Smith's opposition to mercantilism was so strong that he also negated the impact that money had on production even after the original motive for doing so had lost its meaning.

It was for this reason that he and the classical economists that followed him could not admit in their deliberations on value theory that the substance of capital is money and that the risk associated with a money advance was therefore of a monetary nature.[11]

The dismissal of the mercantilists' reflections on the meaning of money and money supply increase contributed a great deal to the inability of the classical theory to withstand the socialist attack on capital as being an instrument for unjust profit in spite of the important mercantilist insight that capital promotes economic growth. This dismissal also led to the loss of the mercantilist perception of capital as a factor of economic promotion tied to its character of money.

[10] See in addition Hans Ch. Binswanger (1993).

[11] Nevertheless, in contrast to their value theory, in the explanation of the market process, Adam Smith and his successors took it completely for granted that profit and interest are monetary figures and all factors of production are to be monetarily compensated. Wesley C. Mitchell points this out when he writes: "Political economy . . . is the science of business, and economic men are money-makers; nevertheless, the use of money is a fact of no importance for economic theory. This seeming contradiction between the letter of the economic law and its spirit as interpreted by loyal commentators long passed without notice. It was part of the classical tradition to accept both views, and not to think of them at the same time" (Mitchell 1950, p. 151).

5.4 Marginal Productivity Theory Versus Net Product or Surplus Theory

For political reasons, the classical labor theory of value could no longer be maintained when it became the instrument of the socialist's exploitations theory. In this situation, the neoclassical marginal productivity theory presented itself as an alternative to the net product or surplus theory. With marginal productivity theory, the question of net product or surplus does not arise, and this, on a purely theoretical level, puts an end to the theory of exploitation.

The marginal productivity theory replaced the net product theory in two stages. In the first stage, the money capital was replaced by "real" capital (equipment, mainly machinery). In the second stage, land was incorporated into "real" capital. Along with it, the "law" of diminishing marginal returns, which had its origins in the practice of land cultivation, was now transferred and applied to "real" capital as a whole. Interest was interpreted as a marginal return of "real" capital.

As a consequence, monetary profit was eliminated by the assumption that, in equilibrium, all factors of production are rewarded by their marginal returns including the marginal return on "real" capital in the form of interest, and these rewards exhaust the total product with nothing left over for gain or profit. This led to the conclusion: There is in equilibrium no profit and, ergo, there is no exploitation.

The change in the definition of the term capital from money capital to "real" capital was introduced in the early nineteenth century by the French classical economist Jean-Baptiste Say (1767–1823). On the one hand, he speaks of capital as an advance, which the capitalist gives himself as an entrepreneur in the form of equity capital in order to achieve a profit for himself, or which he lends to another as borrowed capital for which he is paid interest. On the other hand, however, Say sees production brought about by three productive services (*services productifs*), namely the service of labor, the service of land, and the service of capital. Once a factor of promotion, capital thus became a factor of production.

This redefinition of the term capital by Say was adopted by Walras, who explained the determination of prices as a result of a process of barter. In this process there is no scope for capital as an advance, because there is no time dimension. His somewhat arduous attempts to derive a definition of capital show, however, that in the second half of the nineteenth century it was still not clear how capital should actually be understood. At first, Walras identifies *all* durable goods as capital (Walras 1900, 175ff.). He understands it to be land or real estate (*capitaux fonciers ou terres*), human capital or persons (*capitaux personnels ou personnes*), as well as mobile capital or capital in a more narrow sense (*capitaux mobiliers ou capitaux proprement dits)*. He contrasts capital or durable goods with income or nondurable goods, which he calls income goods (*revenus*), under which he subsumes all goods that could only be used once and then were depleted or ceased to exist. Among these goods he also included raw materials (*matières premières*). Later, however, he exclusively used the term capital for factors of production that were neither land nor persons but rather for the produced means of production, particularly in the form of machinery.

Based on this definition, Philip H. Wicksteed (1844–1927) and John Bates Clark (1847–1938) were the major contributors to the development of the neoclassical marginal productivity theory taking account of the law of diminishing marginal returns. While Wicksteed (1894) was responsible for the microeconomic version, Clark (1931) was responsible for the macroeconomic version. They attempted to explain the distribution of income according to objective standards. Economists are familiar with this explanation, because it is essential part of the conventional economics. The price of each factor of production is equal to its marginal product under the condition of the homogeneity of all units of a production factor, of perfect competition, and finally of general equilibrium with full employment of all factors of production.

With the aid of Euler's theorem, Wicksteed showed that, considering the given assumptions and presupposing a linear homogeneous production function, the total product is divided completely among the production factors (see box p. 67).

In the macroeconomic version formulated by Clark, there are (only) two factors of production, labor and "real" capital. Thus, there are (only) two prices, wages and interest. Consequently, wages are regarded as equal to the marginal product of labor and interest equal to the marginal product of "real" capital, whereby one and the same household can earn income both as employee and as owner of private capital. Clark included natural resources, particularly those of the land, in the "real" capital. But, in fact, by doing so, he makes them disappear. The prices of their services, usually referred to as rents, are considered to be part of the interest. Thus, the overall product is divided up completely—and here Clark follows Wicksteed's formal argumentation—into wages and interest.

In this way, the production function can also be seen as a macroeconomic distribution function. Reading from right to left, a certain amount of real capital services (*K*) and certain amount of labor services (*L*) will produce a certain amount of total production (*Y*). Reading from left to right, it means that total production (*Y*) is completely distributed between labor and capital according to their production input, with nothing left for profit. Thus, the marginal productivity theory can be presented as shown in Fig. 5.1.

Due to the coherence and the simplicity of this theory, it seemed to be a good argument against the exploitation theory of socialism. Clark writes:

> It is the purpose (!) of this work to show that the distribution of the income of society is controlled by a natural law, and that this law, if it worked without friction, would give to every agent of production the amount of wealth which that agent creates. However wages may be adjusted by bargains freely made between individual men, the rates of pay that result from such transactions tend, it is here claimed, to equal that part of the product of industry which is traceable to the labor itself; and however interest may be adjusted by similarly free bargaining, it naturally tends to equal the fractional product that is separately traceable to capital . . . So far as it is not obstructed, it assigns to every one what he has specifically produced. (Clark 1931, V)

If the wages are determined, as Clark says, by "a natural law," it then does not make any difference whether the wages lie above or below the subsistence level or, at any rate, by how much they are above or below it. This renders the thesis

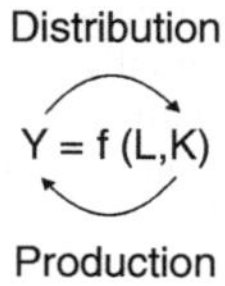

Fig. 5.1 Production and distribution in the neoclassical model

untenable that capitalists exploit workers because they pay them only a subsistence wage. According to the marginal productivity theory, interest is controlled by "a natural law," to the same extent as wages. Any discussion of a "just" distribution becomes irrelevant.[12]

However, the "solution" of the problem of distribution on the basis of the marginal productivity theory led to several problems for the conventional theory. They must either adhere to assumptions which are obviously at odds with reality or introduce assumptions that make them self-contradictory.

Clark, himself, noticed the major problem. It results from the fact that in the macroeconomic production function, "real" capital is treated as a quantity, which is considered, like land, indestructible, even though it actually consists of goods that are being constantly used up and, as a result, must be constantly replaced. Clark seeks to resolve this contradiction with an illustration in which he compares "the" capital with the water power "embodied in an endless succession of drops of falling water" (Clark 1931, p. 121). The water power remains the same even though the individual water drops are different. The invested sum of money, he argues, is nothing more than a symbol for the permanent "real" capital, because, if the entrepreneur speaks of money that he has invested, he assumes that he will retain this money, so that it is as permanent as the water power. Clark's actual words are:

> Why do business men speak of capital in terms of money? Why, if you ask a merchant, "What is your capital?" will he answer, "It is the hundred thousand dollars that I have invested in my shop" It is because what he means by the phrase, a hundred thousand dollars,

[12] See Erich Preiser (1961b, p. 266): "Just as the classical theory opens up to an indictment, the marginal productivity theory tends toward an apology, and not only with John Bates Clark. In the hands of Marx, who was a faithful follower of Ricardo, the classical theory of distribution became a terrible weapon. Ownership of the means of production leads to the owner appropriating portions of the produce of the workers, who are without property, and so, this appropriation is, strictly speaking, robbery, even when done according to the general laws of exchange. This was countered by the marginal productivity theory, most notably by Clark. He examines the laws of income creation. He shows that the amount of return is not only dependent on labor but also on real means of production, which he summarizes as capital including land. So there is not just one factor of production but several—at least two, labor and capital, as the sum of real means of production—, and a portion of the returns inevitably must belong to the owners of these means. For this reason, the income of property is not the appropriation of the wages of others for their labor, but rather a 'rent getter,' a 'product creator.' So, in this way, Clark justified the de facto distribution of income, or at least he thought he justified it."

> is an abiding thing, which he had when he went into business and still has, unless his business has been unfortunate. Yet he is usually under no delusions as to the character of the things that embody his capital; and, in particular, he knows that . . . his productive wealth consists in merchandise, in fixtures, in claims against customers for merchandise sold and delivered, etc. Yet he instinctively and unconsciously thinks and speaks of it as money. (Clark 1931, 118f.)

So, according to Clark, money is nothing else to the entrepreneur than an abstract expression of real goods, which, although they are used up, remain permanent in their entirety. But this view ignores the reality. It is wrong in two ways. *First*, money is nothing abstract to a businessman; on the contrary, it is the one crucial thing that really matters. "Real" capital is only a means to an end. The means and the end should not be confused! The end is an increase of money which shall result from investing money as capital. *Second,* neither "real" capital nor money capital is permanent. The real production goods must be constantly replaced because they are used up (no illustration will ever help get over this consumption no matter how attractive the image of water power manifested in falling drops of water is). But invested money is also not nonperishable per se. It can be lost through inept business practices or unforeseeable changes in the market situation—as Clark himself admits with his reference to possible misfortune of the business—so it is perishable in the sense of being exposed to a risk. But the perishable nature of money capital is totally different from the perishable nature of production goods. In order to ensure that money capital continues to "stay in business," it must flow back by the selling of products yielding profit, which (at least) compensates for the risk. Otherwise the holder of the capital would be better off simply hoarding his money. In contrast, to ensure that real capital stays "in business," replacement investments have to be made on a regular basis. Otherwise it would no longer be ready for production. But these are two completely different things!

Besides, the amount of "real" capital can only be measured by assessing the value of individual "real" capital goods according to their costs in money, but this is only a makeshift solution. It is, as Knut Wicksell had already established, inadmissible, to define the price of the "real" capital as interest and to derive the interest from the marginal productivity of the "real" capital, because the interest is already contained in the costs of the real capital goods. This is an example of premising an argument with its conclusion. Wicksell got it right when he said: "Again, it is futile to attempt . . . to derive the value of capital-goods from their own cost of production or reproduction; for in fact these costs of production include capital and interest . . . We should, therefore, be arguing in a circle".[13]

The contradictions in the theory of capital disappear when we return to the original meaning of capital as a money advance and the profit of the firm as the price of money capital. "Real" capital in terms of produced means of production contributes to the production, but is not part of the distribution of income. In this respect, "real" capital has only an intermediary function. In terms of distribution,

[13] Quoted from Heinz D. Kurz (1999, 157f).

it is a question of the income of the original factors that include—let us repeat it—not only factors of production but also money capital as a factor of promotion. The price of real capital in terms of produced means of production can always be divided into the prices or the incomes of the original factors of production and in the profit of the firm as the price of money capital (See below p. 94).

Another reason for the questionable nature of the marginal productivity theory is the fact that the "law" of diminishing returns cannot be applied adequately to the interaction of labor and "real" capital and, for that reason, is definitely not suited to explain industrial production.

As noted at the start of this section, the "law" of diminishing returns is tied to land. It was formulated, in fact, by considering the interaction between labor and land. Applying the "law" of diminishing returns to "real" capital while virtually eliminating the land can be compared to the grinning Cheshire cat in the children's book *Alice in Wonderland,* which disappears bit by bit until nothing is visible but the cat's disembodied grin, a grin without a cat—the "law" of diminishing returns without land! The relationship between labor and "real" capital (particularly in the form of machinery) is generally fixed in that a specific number of workplaces are assigned to each piece of machinery. In this case, the marginal product cannot be meaningfully defined. In contrast, in agricultural production more workmen can be employed at any time on the same land or more land can be made available to a constant number of workmen, with labor and land being varied in small amounts, thus the "law" of diminishing returns is valid—and only valid—for agricultural production.

This means that while it makes perfectly good sense to use the ceteris paribus clause to explain production in agriculture, that is, to isolate the change of production yield based on the change in one production factor alone, it makes no sense at all to try to use it in explaining industrial production. Here, the factors are simultaneously involved. This means that the marginal product of labor or real capital cannot be constructed in such a manner as to allow a distribution to be derived according to the marginal productivity theory, that is, assuming a variation in one factor alone while the other factors remain constant.

This holds especially true for energy, today's most important factor of production.[14] Energy is essential in running machines. Thus, no marginal product of energy, with machines as a constant, can be determined. For this reason energy does not fit into the neoclassical model. So it was simply dropped. Moreover, the exclusion of energy seemed justified with the argument that the price of energy is low rendering energy costs negligible, and therefore, its contribution to the aggregate product can be ignored. Here it is wrongly assumed that the price of a factor of production indicates its significance in the production process. Reiner Kümmel critically remarked in this context: "In conventional neoclassical theory the energy is . . . neglected altogether . . . or attributed only marginal importance. The argument

[14] See also Thomas Möller (1986).

is that energy's share in total factor cost is small compared to the cost shares of labour and capital. However, the recessions after the oil price crises in 1973/1974 and 1979/1981 have posed the question how a production factor of monetarily minor importance can have such grave economic consequences". (Lindenberger and Kümmel 2002, p. 2, 14)[15]

The deficiencies of the neoclassical marginal productivity theory, however, should not cause us to overlook its principal merit: the emphasis placed on the *diminishing marginal utility* of an (individual) commodity with increased consumption.

The classical economists distinguished between two values, value in use and value in exchange. They were aware that a commodity must have a value in use to have also a value in exchange. However, they saw no connection between the level of value in use and the available quantity. The credit for determining such a connection goes to the neoclassical economists. They recognized that the value of an additional unit of consumer goods—in other words, the marginal utility—is less than the value of a unit of a smaller supply that does not yet include this unit. This results in the necessity to distinguish between the sum of the marginal utility of a commodity at a given amount x and the utility of the total amount x—Walras designated it as the "effective utility". (Walras 1900, p. 76)

The important concept of consumer's rent, which is traced back to Alfred Marshall, is derived from this difference, namely, from the difference of the integral of all marginal utilities, beginning with the highest marginal utility, when only one unit is available, to the lowest marginal utility of the last available unit, and the sum of the marginal utility of the last available unit. Marshall defines the supply available to the consumer to be the amount he can or would be willing to buy at the given price, which indicates the marginal utility of the last available unit. He assumes that "the price which a person pays for a thing can never exceed, and seldom comes up to that which he would be willing to pay rather than go without it: so that the gratification which he gets from its purchase generally exceeds that which he gives up in paying away its price; and he thus derives from the purchase a surplus of pleasure" (Marshall 1890, p. 175). The consumer's surplus can thus be understood as "the excess of the price which he [the consumer] would be willing to pay rather than go without the thing, over that which he actually does pay."

With this approach, it becomes clear that the aggregate monetary income that results from adding the amount of goods and multiplying every good by its price is not identical to the overall utility of the amount of goods. This is to be taken into account when evaluating the distribution of income.

---

[15] See also Herman Daly (2001, p. 12): "Low resource prices are not evidence of nonscarcity and unimportance, but rather a consequence of rapid drawdown leading to increasing technological dependence on a large throughput of cheap resources."

The Marginal Productivity Theory of Distribution

The neoclassical marginal productivity theory is based on the Cobb-Douglas function, a simplified form of a linear homogeneous production function. It takes the following form:

$$P = L^{\alpha}K^{1-\alpha}$$

with

P = social product or national income

L = labor input

K = capital input

α or $1 - \alpha$ is the parameter that measures the output elasticity of the inputs of labor and capital respectively, with $0 < \alpha < 1$.

When the law of diminishing returns is applied under conditions of competition, the costs of the factors of production—wages w and interest r—are equal to their marginal product; thus,

$$w = \frac{\partial P}{\partial L} = \alpha L^{\alpha-1}K^{1-\alpha}$$

and

$$r = \frac{\partial P}{\partial K} = L^{\alpha}(1-\alpha)K^{-\alpha}.$$

The sum of wages W is the product of wage rate and labor input, and the sum of interest R is the product of interest rate and capital input, namely,

$$\begin{aligned} W &= wL \\ &= \alpha L^{\alpha-1}K^{1-\alpha}L \\ &= \alpha L^{\alpha}K^{1-\alpha} \\ &= \alpha P \end{aligned}$$

and

$$\begin{aligned} R &= rK \\ &= L^{\alpha}(1-\alpha)K^{-\alpha}K \\ &= (1-\alpha)L^{\alpha}K^{1-\alpha} \\ &= (1-\alpha)P. \end{aligned}$$

The aggregate income is completely divided up between wages and interests since

$$\begin{aligned} wL + rK &= \alpha P + (1-\alpha)P \\ &= P. \end{aligned}$$

Thus, in this model, the social product is fully distributed to labor in the form of wages and to capital in the form of interests. Wages and interests are determined by the market, based on the technologically given parameter α. Any attempt to increase the share of wages by artificially raising the wage rate would only lead to a lower demand for labor, and unemployment would result. According to this theory, when each factor of production is fully employed, it receives the part of the social product which the "natural law" intended for it.

5.5 The Net Product Theory Rediscovered by Piero Sraffa

While the conventional economic theory is still in line with the neoclassical marginal productivity theory, some economists have taken a second look at the classical net product or surplus theory. The leading exponent of this revival was Piero Sraffa (1898–1983). He started with a general criticism of Marshall's market theory, in his essay "Sulle Relazioni fra Costo e Quantità Prodotta" (Sraffa 1925, 1926). Sraffa (1960) later expanded the classical net product theory or surplus theory into a theory of his own, in his book *Production of Commodities by Means of Commodities*.

Sraffa's theory can be integrated into the classical theory to the extent that he defines, as Urs Weber noted, "the wealth of a society to be the surplus in reproducible goods periodically emerging out of the circular flow of the production process." However, in contrast to the classical theory of economics, his surplus is "virtually identical to the physical surplus of the production system" (Weber 1998, p. 171). This means that the surplus is the same as the total production of the economy minus the purchased goods used in the production process and minus the replacement investments, in other words, the same as the national income. According to Sraffa, this is divided between only two factors of production, labor and capital. By including wages in the surplus, Sraffa takes into account the fact that wages had risen substantially higher than the subsistence level since the early nineteenth century. The only thing left of the classical teachings on subsistence wages is the observation that there should be a minimum wage because workers, in any case, must be paid enough to survive. Another difference to the classical theory in Sraffa's theory is that wages as well as profit are to be paid *after* completion of the production process. Because workers are paid at the end of the production period and not at the beginning, this makes capital unnecessary as an advance. In fact, Sraffa understands capital to be "real" capital in the sense of produced means of production, not as a factor of promotion. Here, Sraffa is approaching the neoclassical theory. However, the profit is not determined, as is the case in the latter, by the marginal product of "real" capital but rather by the level of the money rate of interest. Concerning this, Sraffa makes the following statement: "The rate of profits, as a ratio, has a significance which is independent of any prices, and can be 'given' before the prices are fixed. It is accordingly susceptible of being determined from outside the system of products, in particular being determined by the level of the money rate of interest" (Sraffa 1960, p. 33). In this way, a connection is established between the real and the monetary spheres of economics, which is missing in the neoclassical theory.

Sraffa concentrates on replacing one of the concepts central to the neoclassic theory, namely the determination of the prices of the factors of production based on their marginal productivity. Instead he puts forward a theory of his own explaining the interdependency of the prices of all products and factors of production by technically fixed coefficients of production (except the rate of interest). Bertram Schefold writes in his mathematical exposition of Sraffa's analysis of joint production: "It is Sraffa's great merit to have developed [Ricardo's] fundamental concept of value in classical theory into a coherent logical system that provides a real alternative to the marginalists' theory of prices" (Schefold 1971, p. 11).

Even if Sraffa did not continue with the dynamic approach of the classical theory, he still adopted essential elements of it, making it relevant to newer developments in production theory. In particular, it provides the basis for the "Theory of Production" by Heinz D. Kurz and Neri Salvadori, in which "the prices are taken to fulfill the condition of *reproduction*: they allow producers to cover just costs of production (including, as things may be, the provisions of the producers and profits at the 'ordinary' rate of return on the value of capital advanced at the beginning of the uniform period of production)" (Kurz and Salvadori 1995, p. 1, emphasis added by the author). This theory is embedded in a comprehensive description of the development of theories of production or reproduction.[16]

5.6 The Historical School and Its Further Development: Alternative Contributions to the Theory of Production

The historical school of economics gained influence, particularly in Germany, in (partial) opposition to classical economics, pointing out that the economy is always embedded in historical time. Admittedly, the historical school often placed too much emphasis on the historical context, concluding that it is impossible to comprehend the economy with formal models. With this conclusion, the historical school went a step too far with this skepticism. Nevertheless it is important to incorporate the impact of this school on the economic theory in order to take into account aspects of reality that can only be understood by referring to the historical context.[17] We will identify a few of these insights, while taking the further development of this school into account under the key terms institutionalism, evolutionary economics, and ecological economics.

Karl Knies (1821–1898), the leading theorist of the "older" historical school, declared in his major work *Die Politische Ökonomie vom geschichtlichen Standpunkt* that "economic facts are almost meaningless for economics when their findings are not accompanied by a special determination of the causes of which they are the result" (Knies 1883, p. 468).[18] By pointing out the causality, Knies draws attention to the sequence of time because the cause of a phenomenon always precedes the phenomenon in time. This Kniesian version is in direct

[16] See also the article by Luigi Pasinetti on "The Sraffa-enigma: Introduction" (2005), in the *European Journal of the History of Economic Thought*'s special issue on Sraffa, as well as the lectures that were given at the Piero Sraffa conference 2003 in Rome.

[17] For a comprehensive survey of the Historical school, refer to the essay by Heinz Rieter (1994), who concisely summarizes its main ideas.

[18] See also Jürgen Löwe (1998, p. 64).

opposition to the neoclassic theory that explains economic relationships in terms of functional relationships in which all magnitudes are in simultaneous mutual interdependence.[19]

Sequential time also finds expression in the notion of economic stages, which was a particular concern of the historical school. Different fundamental principles apply in each of the different stages. Bruno Hildebrand (1812–1878), who, after Knies and Wilhelm Roscher (1817–1894), was the third representative of the "older" historical school, understands economic development as a process proceeding in three consecutive stages, "barter economy, money economy, and credit economy," in the sense of "three possible forms of exchange" and writes: "The natural barter economy presupposes economic conditions in which capital is not yet an independent force capable of nationwide production. . . . Land holdings and manpower are therefore the only sources of wealth. . . . It was the money economy that gradually alleviated this deficiency" (Hildebrand 1922, p. 336, 341, 343).

Karl Bücher (1847–1931), an exponent of the "younger" historical school, also distinguishes three stages, but he chooses the length of a product's path from producer to consumer as the determining criterion. (Bücher 1914) He speaks of three stages of development with varying degrees of division of labor. The first is the "closed domestic economy," in which indigenous production dominates and people live from their own products; the second is the "town economy," in which enterprises only produce goods according to the customers' orders; and the third, the "national economy" or "world economy," in which companies dominate that produce goods to sell on the market.

Hildebrand's and Bücher's stages correspond to a large extent, which can be seen when we combine Hildebrand's second and third stages—his money and credit economies on the one side—and Bücher's first and second stages—the closed domestic and the town economies on the other side. We can do this because Bücher's national or world economy, which is his third stage, is a money and credit economy as Hildebrand understands it.

A major insight of the historical school was the observation that fixed costs arise when machinery become a part of the production process and that fixed costs have a decreasing impact on the unit costs the greater the amount produced: The unit costs or the average cost drops with increased production. When the unit costs or average costs are lowered, it also becomes possible to lower the prices so that larger volumes can be sold.

Karl Bücher worked out this insight and summarized it in a "law of mass production." It is interesting to note that Bücher especially points out that when the price is already very low and, because of that, demand is already high, it is not worthwhile to lower the price any further according to the reductions in unit costs.

[19] This assessment is also true of the classical school. See also Heinrich Bortis: "Time plays a crucial role in classical-keynesian political economy which is . . . *essentially historical*. Objectively given causal forces by applied or real-type causal models are historical by nature since the process of causation . . . goes on in historical time" (Bortis 1997, p. 118).

In this case, profit increases per unit. Bücher denotes this profit as the "priority rent of mass production." It makes mass production even more appealing.

In order to correctly understand the "law of mass production," we must compare it to the "economies of scale" discussed in conventional economy and often mistakenly identified with the "law of mass production." When explaining "economies of scale," a neoclassic homogeneous production function is assumed with the two factors labor and "real" capital. The only difference to the otherwise imputed linear homogeneous production function is that by increasing the use of both factors of production, the production (P) increases overproportionately with the input of both factors. The production function, therefore, has a nonlinear nature and is seen as being with λ as parameter:

$$\lambda^n P = f(\lambda L, \lambda K) \quad \text{with} \quad n > 1.$$

In contrast, it is assumed in the "law of mass production" as formulated by Bücher that only the input of one factor of production, namely, that of machinery, that is, "real" capital, increases, while the input of the other factor of production, labor, decreases:

$$\frac{\mathrm{d}K}{\mathrm{d}t} > 0,$$

$$\frac{\mathrm{d}L}{\mathrm{d}t} < 0.$$

This means that, in contrast to the neoclassical theory, labor is not substituted by "real" capital within the frame of the *same* production function. It rather presupposes the transition *from one production function to another*. In this sense, the "law of mass production" is not compatible with the neoclassical "economies of scale."

Another important element in the historical approach was the understanding that the focus of economic activity depends on legal conditions and thereby on state regulations, emphasized by the American school of institutional economics, or the so-called institutionalism. Above all, this theory includes the regulation of banking and finance. In his last book, *Absentee Ownership*, Thorstein Veblen (1857–1929), who is considered to be the preeminent exponent of institutionalism, stresses the significance of financing and its development. He explained the expansion of industrial capitalism and the growth of production with the "larger use of credits" based on institutional reforms in banking in the United States in the 1920s (Veblen 1923, pp. 326–397).[20] A substantial increase in this money and credit expansion resulted from the suspension of the gold standard and, in consequence, from the unlimited possibility of creating money in the form of paper money and bank

[20] See Lukas Hagen (2002, p. 20): "In *Absentee Ownership,* Veblen notes this general consolidation and spreading of montetary thinking, which is an absolutely necessary condition for thinking in the category of profit-oriented property and the general credit financing of economic activities."

money through granting credits. This is very precisely described by John R. Commons (1862–1945), next to Veblen the most frequently mentioned representative of institutionalism:

> When the gold standard was suspended by England in September, 1931, and later by the United States in 1933, there remained the existing method of creating money by private negotiations at the commercial banks, to be used as checking accounts by depositors. This kind of money "deposits," was not a deposit literally in the old warehouse meaning of a deposit of physical things like gold or silver. Instead, the deposits were banker's debts "past due," and therefore not bearing interest, but created outright in order to purchase the debts of business men "not yet due," and to bear interest until the future date when due. These debts of bankers not bearing interest became, directly or indirectly, the whole of modern money. (Commons 1956, p. 239)

Based on the findings of Veblen and Commons, Wesley C. Mitchell (1874–1948), who is usually mentioned as the third most important exponent of institutionalism, draws attention to the necessity of placing money at the center of economic theory in his book "The Backward Art of Spending Money":

> The current tendency to make money the center around which economics science clusters', then, is a tendency to be fostered. For that course promises (1) to clarify economic theory by giving it a better framework, (2) to render economic theory more useful by directing attention to those actual processes with which all serious proposals for governmental regulation and social reorganization must deal, (3) to make economics more realistic and therefore more interesting intellectually as well as practically, and finally (4) to make economic theory more profound by orienting the economics for a fruitful study of this aspect of human behavior. (Mitchell 1950, p. 176)

The knowledge accumulated by the historical school and institutionalism has been expanded upon within the framework of evolutionary economics—particularly in the second half of the twentieth century. Evolutionary economics is not, however, a unified theory but rather a number of theories primarily distinguished by the fact that they distance themselves from neoclassic economics by emphasizing the historical dimensions of fundamental economic principles, even if individual authors underscore the distance from neoclassic economics to different degrees. Instead of looking for one—*the one*—economic law, they seek to explain economic principles in historical and causal sequence. The primary concern, as Kurt Dopfer (2001, p. 4) points out, is "the second major question of the classical research agenda: the evolution of the economic system. In terms of the history of economic thought, it can be linked with the models of the historical school, institutionalism and other 'evolutionary' strands in economics." In contrast to institutionalism, however, monetary aspects are not studied within the framework of evolutionary economics. Instead, the actual basic principles of production are dealt with in depth. The most important principle, as Carsten Herrmann-Pillath (2001) argues, is the universal balance of energy as an ontological category because, "unless there is a continuous supply of energy, living systems will display decay of structures and loss of stored information. Therefore the last conceptual building block of our ontological principles for evolutionary economics is energy as the most universal constraint for the production and conservation of information" (Herrmann-Pillath 2001, p. 115).

A constant energy input is not enough, however, to ensure further development. It must be supplemented by the production of "novelty" with the aid of the human brain, or one could say, with the aid of the human imagination, as Ulrich Witt (2001) stresses: "The different strands of evolutionary economics, all of which put innovations in the center stage, indeed agree, more or less explicitly, on the crucial role which novelty plays in economic change" (Witt 2001, p. 49). The conditions favoring the creation of innovations must, as Witt further emphasizes, always allow room for unexpected developments; otherwise, if innovations were known about beforehand, they would not be innovations. Accordingly, the dynamic of the economy is always an unforeseeable, open dynamic—in contrast to the neoclassical world, in which complete information prevails. "If the future dynamics are contingent on the not yet known specific informational content of novelty, the assumption of a dynamic system with a known, uniquely determined, solution would clearly be a misconception" (Witt 2001, p. 50). For that reason, only the prerequisites for the creation of innovations can be incorporated into fundamental economic principles, not their content.[21]

With this reference to the entropy law, a connection is established between evolutionary economics and ecological economics, in which the law of entropy forms the most important point of reference.[22] N. Georgescu-Roegen (1971) laid the basis for this when he incorporated the second law of thermodynamics into economics.[23] Entropy develops over time. It is irreversible and thus a sequential linear process. Ecological economics is based on the scarcity resulting in accordance with the entropy law, since, as Herman E. Daly, who can be considered the founder of ecological economics, emphasizes: "The entropy law is the basic physical coordinate of scarcity" (Daly 1977, p. 16).[24] This scarcity is not to be understood to be the shortfall of the available means of production at a specific point in time as in the neoclassical theory, but rather as the scarcity of the "world," that only becomes apparent over the course of historical time. It is ultimately the result of the limited amount of universally available energy. Entropy counteracts the unlimited growth of the national product and therefore implies an end of time—although not in the sense of final days of the "world" because, thanks to solar radiation, plant growth is secure and with it a food supply for at least a limited population of animals and mankind but rather in the sense of the final days of wealth.[25]

---

[21] For a survey on the development of evolutionary economics, see Giovanni Dosi and Richard R. Nelson (1994), as well as Marco Lehmann-Waffenschmidt (2001). For an overview of the general fundamentals of evolutionary economics, see Kurt Dopfer (2005).

[22] The connection of evolutionary economics and ecological economics is particularly highlighted by Joseph A. Weissmahr (2001).

[23] See also Mathias Binswanger (1992).

[24] For more information on entropy law as an economic category, see Costanza et al. (1997), and Malte Faber et al. (1996).

[25] For an overview of the development of ecological economics, see Martin Held (2005).

In summarizing the findings of the historical school and its further developments, it should be particularly noted that sequential time as a prerequisite for causal explanations and the embedding of economic processes in institutional settings that change over time are to be taken into account. This opens up a whole series of doors particularly for the explanation of the process of economic growth, its prerequisites and its consequences—doors left closed by the timeless neoclassical models.

5.7 Conclusion

Our review of the development of the theory of production leads to the conclusion that marginal productivity theory is not a suitable alternative to the physiocratic, mercantilist, and classical net product theory. By ignoring capital as a factor of promotion, and by ignoring land and natural resources including energy, the neoclassic theory led the theory of production into a blind alley. There is only one way out of a blind alley and that is to return back. We must return back to the net product or surplus theory based on the physiocratic, mercantilist, and classical approaches. This implies the redefining of capital as a factor of promotion and the inclusion of nature in the economic theory.

Moreover, the institutional and ecological conditions, as required by historically oriented economics, must also be considered in the explanation of production and distribution.

Discarding the marginal productivity theory should be easier today insofar as there is no longer the need for an argument against the socialist exploitation theory, since the workers, who have essentially become employees nowadays, are clearly major participants of the net product or surplus. Sraffa already took this into account in his version of the net product theory. We can no longer speak of a general exploitation of labor as it was derived from the socialistic interpretation of the classical theory. This insight should clear the way towards the recognition of both, the net product or surplus as the core of economic wealth and the distribution of the net product or the surplus to all factors of production *and* to capital as a factor of promotion.

6 Production Involving Nature and Imagination

6.1 Production on a Limited Scale: Traditional Agriculture as a Basis for the Neoclassical Model of a Robinson Crusoe Economy

Because traditional agriculture was the embodiment of the economy, it is important to understand the development of the modern economy and to explain how much the process of industrialization and the process of growth have changed the economy since it was based on traditional agriculture.

This task is easy in so far as we already have a model of traditional agriculture that is described very precisely. It is the Robinson Crusoe model, which was and is the basis for the neoclassical and the conventional theory of production. So all we have to do is to describe the essential characteristics of this model to recognize how production in the modern economy differs from it. This will show how far a new theory of production seeking to explain the modern economy must distance itself from the neoclassical and, therefore, from the conventional theory.

The following are the main characteristics of the Robinson Crusoe model, which are also true for traditional agriculture:

- Robinson Crusoe took possession of the land he worked as the result of a shipwreck, an event that lies beyond economic consideration. It is simply a fact. Therefore, no legal sanction of ownership is required. It is obvious that Robinson Crusoe can reserve the fruit of the land and his labor for himself since he is the only inhabitant of the island. Institutional regulations are not necessary. This corresponds to the situation of traditional agriculture, since the land of most of the farmers was occupied in ancient times and has since been passed on to the descendents in accordance with traditional inheritance laws. This means the land was allocated to each farmer for historical reasons and, therefore, by chance, just as Robinson Crusoe being stranded on "his" island was by chance. The traditional farmer—we are thinking here of the independent farmer—lives also like Robinson Crusoe with the certainty that the fruits of his labor in the fields, which

H.C. Binswanger, *The Growth Spiral*, DOI 10.1007/978-3-642-31881-8_6,

he owns and cultivates, belong to him. He can reserve them completely for himself. In this situation, there is no need to discuss institutional regulations.

- For both Robinson Crusoe and the traditional farmer, land is the sole basis for natural production. It is in short supply and therefore must be managed economically. Other resources such as sunlight and air are free goods. They belong to no one and are available in abundance. For that reason, they can be left out of economic calculation.
- The land or the soil's fertility is a regenerative or renewable resource. That means it is available for production year after year on an ongoing basis, provided it is not overused. However, it is to be assumed that both Robinson Crusoe and the traditional farmer refrain from such an overuse—regardless of whether it would be technically possible at all—because both know that he would sacrifice the basis of their existence. In their own interest, they will adhere to sustainable management. Therefore, the regenerative capabilities of the soil are always maintained. There is also no environmental pollution, and no special effort is needed to clean up. Nature cleans itself.
- Robinson Crusoe, as well as the traditional farmer, can determine himself how much he wants to work under the given conditions, that is with a limited area of land and sustainable farming methods. In this, he only needs to consider the "law" of diminishing marginal product. This "law" is based on the experience in land cultivation. The crop yield first increases proportionally to the use of labor, then increases less proportionally and finally does not increase at all. This can be explained by the simple fact that plants need space to develop and to take advantage of ecological cycles. The available land, therefore, becomes a limiting factor in the production. For this reason land's input to the production can, ultimately, not be offset by an increased input of labor, no matter how large the increase will be.
- An optimal input of labor results from a trade-off between the marginal utility of the worker's product and the marginal disutility or pain of work. In view of the fact that the day has only 24 h and man needs his rest, it is natural to assume that, as the workday approaches the 24-h day, the marginal disutility of work increases. Given these conditions, it is obvious that Robinson Crusoe and the traditional farmer would stretch out the workday (only) so far until the marginal utility of the worker's product is equal to the marginal disutility of work. This leads to an equilibrium, in which Robinson Crusoe or the traditional farmer can be considered fully employed.
- It can also be assumed that the production yield that Robinson Crusoe realizes with optimal use of labor, that is, in equilibrium, is large enough to guarantee at least a minimum subsistence. If this were not the case, Robinson Crusoe, or the traditional farmer, would not have survived. Accordingly, we can assume that the settlement of a country in traditional agriculture has progressed to the point that the subsistence minimum will be provided even by the marginal land, that is, the least productive piece of land that has been settled. Any land less productive will not be settled. For this reason, the absolute amount of the production need not be discussed any further. Suffice it to say that the homo oeconomicus—be it

Robinson Crusoe or the traditional farmer—produces an optimal yield under the given conditions.

- Over time, Robinson Crusoe and the traditional farmer can increase to a certain extent the production capacity and the productivity of their labor with the aid of investments, such as improving the condition of the soil, building sheds, and producing new tools. But they can only do this by foregoing a corresponding amount of consumption and thus saving, because in the time he works for the investment goods, he cannot work for the production of consumer goods. Inasmuch as consumption primarily serves for satisfying hunger, which can be assumed to be the case both for Robinson Crusoe and the traditional farmer, commodities available only at some date in the future are of less value than commodities that are immediately available. Therefore, the values of future goods are discounted by a certain percentage. Saving and investing occur only when the good's additional value exceeds this discounting. Furthermore, it must also be taken into account that the soil's productivity can only be increased to a limited degree through investments. So the marginal value of the investment projects will become less with each additional project undertaken. The investment activities will end when the marginal efficiency of the investment has decreased to the level of the discounting factor applying to future goods. This limits the amount by which, through saving and investing, the yield can be increased in both the Robinson Crusoe economy and traditional agriculture.
- The Robinson Crusoe economy integrates production and consumption within one economic unit, as in agricultural households. Both produce the goods that they need themselves. Thus, no capital is needed to establish a firm. Under these circumstances, there is no scope for profit or interest that would compensate for the risk of capital investment. Whatever is produced is for the benefit of Robinson or the farmer himself.
- Robinson Crusoe, or the traditional farmer, has no need of money as a means of payment because he is producing for himself. But even if he were in contact with a few other "Robin Crusoes" on neighboring islands or with neighboring farmers, an exchange of goods could be settled by means of barter. At best, money would be used as a means of accounting.

All these characteristics are the main ingredients of the neoclassical model. In this model, there is no need to discuss the institutional settings. They are self-evident. The economic activities tend to an optimal use of scarce resources under the regime of decreasing marginal utilities of the consumption of goods and the increasing marginal costs of the production of goods. All resources are renewable. They renew themselves in such a way that they neither increase nor decrease in their amount. The number of goods and the preferences of the consumers do not change; they are fixed.

All physically scarce resources are appropriated by an owner, with the consequence that physical scarcity is identical with economic scarcity. As the market is, in principle, understood as barter between mainly self-sufficient households that exchange only surplus products, no money is needed other than as unit of account.

This confirms what we have pointed out already: The neoclassical model, upon which the conventional model is based, is not the product of (overly) abstract thinking, as is often claimed, but rather a valid description of an economic system, albeit an economic system that belongs to the past. Therefore, the issue is not just to adapt an abstract model to reality but to *replace* a model based on an outdated Robinson Crusoe or agrarian reality by a model explaining the reality of the modern industrialized economy. This economy is open to continuous change. Its dynamics are in complete contrast to the static character of the neoclassical model.

6.2 The Expansion of the Resource Base in the Modern Economy

The use of natural resources and the human capacity of imagination are continually being augmented in the modern economy, expanding both production as well as the variety of products. Manpower is being complemented as well as replaced by energy. New opportunities for investment projects are continually opening up. Therefore, the "law" of diminishing marginal returns, the "law" of increasing disutility of work, and the assumption of a given ranking of investments with diminishing marginal efficiency are no longer valid in the modern economy. The "law" of diminishing marginal utility applies only to individual products and no longer to all products as a whole because the number of products is constantly increasing.

While all of the economic restraints due to scarcity caused Robin Crusoe and the farmers in traditional agriculture to economize the use of available resources, in the modern economy of today there are strong incentives for producers to overcome these scarcity restraints. *This is the basic difference between the production goals set in the modern economy and the production goals set by Robinson Crusoe and the traditional farmer*. It is no longer a matter of optimally balancing the benefits of labor's product against the disutility of work effort within the limits of fixed amounts of resources and the restriction of time. Rather, it is a matter of expanding the access to natural resources by appropriating them and intensifying the access to them with the help of human imagination. This appropriation is supported by the process of money creation and the use of an ever-increasing amount of money for the exploration and exploitation of the natural resources.

Therefore, the concept of equilibrium loses its meaning in the sense of a situation that, lacking outside influences, constantly repeats itself. The modern economy develops not toward optimization but toward progressive maximization.

There is a continuous appropriation of resources. This can take place in two ways: either by direct access during the act of production itself or through an allocation of ownership *prior to* and independent of the act of production.

The first case involves the appropriation of natural goods or resources that, as such, are almost intangible and therefore are difficult to allocate. Examples are air or sunlight, as well as those natural goods or resources that could be allocated, but have not been allocated till today, such as wild plants and animals, the landscape, the primeval forests, and the oceans. In both cases, we speak of free goods or free resources. These goods or resources are only appropriated through their use in the production process, for example, when farmers make use of sunlight for their plants because the latter will not grow without it, or when factory owners make use of air because their production depends on oxygen, or when hotel owners make use of the landscape to sell the view along with overnight stays.

The second case involves the appropriation of tangible natural goods or resources that can be and also are allocated. Through appropriation they become economic goods or economic resources. They can be sold independent of the production of commodities, where these resources are used as inputs. In this way, a separate market can be created for them. Ownership of natural goods or natural resources includes two legal rights:

- First, the right of exclusive use of the goods or resources
- Second, the right of disposal over the goods and the resources itself in terms of selling, leasing, renting, and mortgaging.

The *right of exclusive use* was already present in traditional agriculture. There, the deciding factor of ownership is that the producer is able to reserve the goods he produces for himself.

The *right of disposal* makes ownership the basis of the market because only ownership provides the right to offer a resource or a good on the market. The owner is the supplier. And, vice versa, the supplier can be assumed to be the owner. He can decide whether or not he wants to offer the resources or goods on the market and, if so, at what price he wants to offer them.

In this way, ownership creates both abundance and scarcity. It creates abundance because, without the right to claim ownership of products derived from appropriated resources, continuous production would never take place at all. The alternative would be living hand to mouth. On the other hand, ownership creates a scarcity for the nonowners because they can acquire resources or goods on the market only if they pay a price for them.

In this context it must be noted that scarcity in the market is not the same as a physical scarcity of resources or goods because non-appropriated resources or goods can become physically scarce without a rise in price, since they have no owner who can ask a price for them. Conversely, natural commodities found in physical abundance can become in short supply on the market if they are appropriated and their owners demand a price for them.

Therefore, in contrast to the Robinson Crusoe economy or the traditional agriculture, physical shortage and shortage in the market can widely differ.

The expansion of the scope of production is associated with an increase in restitution costs. These are the costs that must be paid to maintain the basis for further production.

Restitution costs in the Robinson Crusoe economy and in the traditional agriculture are only a matter of covering the necessities for surviving of the laborer, because the maintenance of the natural basis of production is always assured in that only renewable resources are used and a sustainable method of production is assured. In the modern economy, it is different. Restitution costs must also be provided for the maintenance of the natural basis of production:

- First, for the restitution of renewable resources if they are overused (e.g., for reforestation), or for the eventual changeover to substitutes that are more abundantly available (e.g., for desalination of seawater)
- Second, for a continuing exploration of nonrenewable resources that get scarce on the one side or recycling and changeover to substitutes on the other side
- Third, for closing regional or local supply gaps through new transport routes or supply lines with a corresponding geographical redistribution of the utilization of resources.

If the corresponding restitution action is not taken, external costs in terms of *losses* will have to be accepted. These will be dubbed *loss costs*. What is meant here are reductions in production potential, which will lead to the inability to further offer certain goods because the specific resource needed for their production is no longer available. Such loss costs arise when no restitution is possible technically, when the resources belong to no one, that is, no owner exists to provide for their maintenance out of self-interest, or if the owner himself has no interest in their long-term preservation because he is only interested in a short-term perspective.

Hence, in the modern economy, the costs for the restitution of the productive power of natural resources must be added to the restitution costs for the maintenance of manpower, that is, for the survival of the laborer, in consideration of the lost costs.

In the following paragraphs, we will consider the magnitude of the potential for expanding the scope of production taking into account the services of nature, and what effect it will have on the growth potential of the economy.

In the modern economy, nature is involved in the production process in various ways. Considering this, the term "land" is too limited when speaking of nature. Instead, each specific natural resource and its specific contribution to the production should be recognized.

Doing so, we must distinguish between, first, an active involvement of the resource as power; second, a passive involvement of the resource as material being processed in the production; and, third, an involvement of the resource as the location or site of an economic activity without being involved in the production process itself. Accordingly, we can speak of an *active function*, *of* a *material function,* and of a *location function* of nature. Some resources are involved in the production process with all three functions and others with two or only one function. However, we must always keep all three functions separate in order to be able to understand the dynamics of nature's participation in the production process.

With this aspect in mind, it is important to distinguish three categories of natural resources, namely:

- Renewable or regenerative resources, whose supply is constantly replenished after their use if they are not overexploited
- Nonrenewable or non-regenerative resources, whose use can be increased from one period to the next by exploration and exploitation but whose absolute amount is reduced by their use

- Location resources that serve (simply) as production or transport sites, whose amount is not reduced by the use, but that are subject to conflicts of use.

In the following, we will consider the three categories separately, whereby it will be necessary to subdivide them further according to certain aspects.

The *renewable* or *regenerative resources* were the original basis of economy. Their active and material functions are closely connected.

The most important renewable resource is land, as soil that can be cultivated by farming. It produces by cultivation a yield many times over what the uncultivated land would produce. However, cultivation and maintenance costs occur.

Also included among the renewable resources are the forests that provide lumber, the steppes and the alpine pastures that serve as grazing land, and all of the wild animals that are hunted and the fish that are caught. The use of these resources consists essentially in extracting an amount, which should regenerate every year with no (or little) human support.

Another renewable resource is freshwater that is constantly renewing itself in the hydrologic cycle. To be used, it just needs to be directed into appropriate canals or extracted in the sense of collected or drawn from a well.

Let us now take a closer look at these three types of renewable resources with respect to their potential for their increasing use in the process of economic growth.

The *cultivation of land* has its origin in the Neolithic age, 10,000 or more years ago. The original appropriation took place through the settlement of unclaimed land and subsequent sanctioning through state regulation—today by way of an entry in a land registry. Most of the land in the world has now been claimed. Exceptions are only lands not yet completely seized and distributed, for example, primeval forests, steppes, and high mountains, as well as new land resulting from dyke building or from the draining of wetlands.

If agricultural production can be hardly expanded any more by the acquisition of additional land, it is still possible through intensifying the use of the land. Although the "law" of diminishing marginal product of labor defines a limit to the use of additional labor, it does not for the mechanization of agriculture, the use of fertilizers and pesticides, the conversion to hydroculture, the breeding of plants with higher yields, the use of genetic engineering, etc. However, the intensification of production carries the risk of endangering the fertility of the soil and the quality of the plants produced. Moreover, one should note that all regenerative resources require time to regenerate, and as a result, their use cannot be arbitrarily accelerated.

All in all, however, the possibilities for expansion still seem to prevail. Hence, the use of the land farming still makes a considerable contribution to the net product in a growing economy—with reservations concerning the aforementioned risks.

The same does not hold true for the use of the *rest of the renewable resources*—mainly forests, pasture lands, fish, and wild animals—that are exploited through simple extraction. They cannot be seized and controlled by an owner in the same way as land used for farming and are, therefore, subject to the danger of over-exploitation and depletion (see Hardin 1968). In order to ensure their sustainable management, these resources were often made subject to special arrangements—though not everywhere and only to a certain extent. The purpose of these arrangements is to reduce the exploitation to the extent that they can always regenerate.[1] The stock usually belongs to either a cooperative or to the state, which has control over it through the granting of exclusive rights, for example, for logging, grazing, and fishing or hunting to the members of a cooperative or the owner of a license issued by the state. These rights of use are restricted rights. They often include an obligation of maintenance as well.[2]

These special arrangements result in the yield being sustainable in the long run, provided the special provisions are actually enforced. However, the possibilities of increases in the yield are limited because of these arrangements. If these arrangements are not enforced, the opposite is true. The yield will increase rapidly, but the stock will be dramatically reduced due to overexploitation.

For this reason, the contribution of these resources in furthering economic growth is minimal. Although non-sustainable methods can lead to short-term spurts of growth, the result is that either major restitution costs become necessary, for example, for reforestation, or loss costs have to be accepted if no restitution is undertaken.

Freshwater as drinking and process water is a completely different matter. Aside from soil, water is the most important natural resource. It has the great advantage of never being depleted as a whole. All used freshwater flows off somewhere, falls again from the clouds as rain.[3] But world's total supply of freshwater is limited, making overexploitation possible. This results in a lowering of the groundwater level. The water supply is particularly liable to dwindle where it is used the most, in major cities and in large-scale agriculture. This creates the need to replenish the supply by channeling freshwater from areas where it is still in abundance. In principle, it is also possible to desalinate sea water. But this leads to high restitution costs. If restitution action is not taken or consumption is not constrained, a permanent shortage of water may be the result.

A small part of freshwater was and is traditionally in private ownership, such as the well on one's own land or water from a cistern. But the larger part of the water is

[1] See Pearce and Turner (1990).

[2] An interesting form of sustainable management is the informal system of social insurance practiced in fishing communities in Polynesia. It consists of the fisherman sharing the portion of his catch that exceeds his own needs with relatives and neighbors. In turn, he becomes the recipient of such surplus, if his catch is insufficient to feed his family. At the same time, care is taken not to overfish the fishing grounds. In a case study of fishing in the village of Lofanga in the Kingdom of Tonga, Andrea Bender, Wolfram Kägi, and Ernst Mohr (2002) show how such a sustainable strategy works. The sustainability of this social insurance system comes into better focus when the same authors present another village, called Uikan, in the Kingdom of Tonga, where this system became completely eroded after an Australian expert had advised the fishermen to increase their catch by organizing themselves into fishing clubs and by fishing more often and with larger boats. They sell their catch to the owners of the boats, who, in turn, sell them on the city markets. The result is a clearly discernable overexploitation of the fishing grounds. The system of mutual insurance still exists there in only a rudimentary form, if at all.

[3] An exception is the use of water that has been "stored" in the strata deep in the earth and is now being brought up.

in public hands. Thus, the state can charge a price for water's use in the form of taxes that will finance its processing and the wastewater drainage systems. But in general, the taxes are too low to restrict the consumption of water. For some time now, however, the supplying of water has been increasingly privatized. As far as this is the case, its price becomes a market price that will take local water scarcity into account. Prices can rise to an extent that the consumption may be reduced. But then, industrial and agricultural use is given preference because the user can easily afford to pay the higher price. In consequence, there is the threat that the possibility of using water for drinking and common purposes will be negatively affected.

Summarising, it can be said that freshwater literally falls from the sky. Its contribution to the economy's net product is still enormous, but its future contribution to economic growth is minor because its use is reaching its limit in one way or another. The conflict about water use may become one of the major problems resulting from economic growth.

In addition to the renewable resources, the *mining of nonrenewable resources* has, since early times, played a certain, if only subordinate, role. In the Paleolithic, Mesolithic, and Neolithic ages, it was predominately flint. The Bronze Age followed in the second millennium BC, in which tools and vessels were produced from bronze, an alloy of copper and tin. Bronze was essentially replaced by iron in the first millennium BC, which is why it is referred to as the Iron Age.

Energy gained from nature has been also used since antiquity in transport as well as in production. Yet it was not extracted from deposits in the earth but rather gathered or collected on the surface of the land and above, namely, wind (sailing, windmills), water (rafts, watermills), and since the sixteenth century more and more charcoal.

But only since the industrial revolution that began with the invention of the steam engine in the eighteenth century the use of nonrenewable resources became dominant in the economy. It was founded on raw materials such as iron, copper, tin, and all the other metals, particularly aluminum, and chemical raw materials, as well as on energy produced from mineral resources, chief among them lignite and bituminous coal, crude oil, and natural gas.

Mineral resources are not considered to be open to occupation as land originally was. Ownership of deposits has been and is dependent upon permits or concessions from the state. The owner has also to pay so-called royalties. In this way, the state has a share in the profits of the exploitation.

Geologists distinguish between two categories of stocks: "resources" and "reserves." This differentiation also has economic relevance. The earth's total supply of existing discovered and not yet discovered and assessed deposits of raw material or of energy sources is termed "resources." Their magnitude is estimated or assumed with the help of geological methods. "Reserves," on the other hand, are understood to be the amount of discovered, that is, explored and with available technology and at acceptable costs exploitable deposits. This amount is reduced by exploitation and increased by exploration and technical progress. In addition, the reserves can be supplemented by hitherto unknown or unused resources.

The dynamics of resources exploitation is depicted in Fig. 6.1.

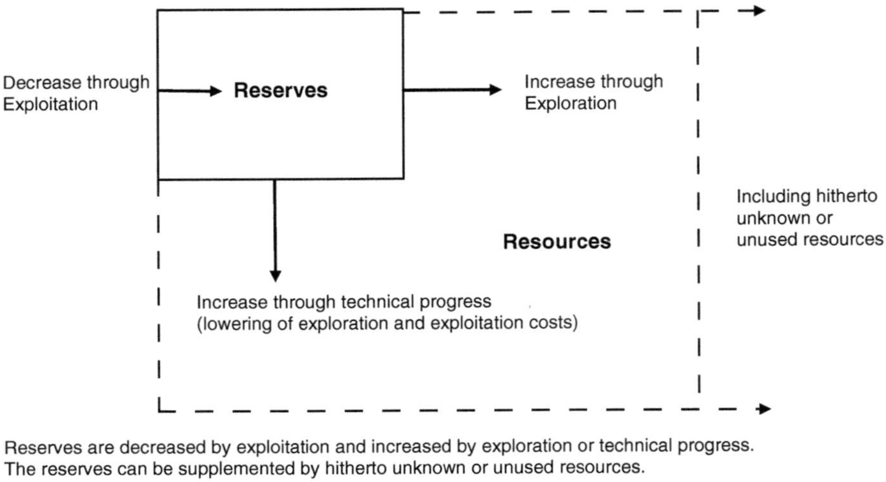

Fig. 6.1 The dynamics of resource exploitation

The known "reserves" for most of the resources are (still) increasing over the course of time.

Exploration is a prerequisite for establishing ownership because something can only be owned if its quantity is known. Therefore, only the explored deposits, the "reserves," have an owner, who can offer the raw materials and the energy on the market. For this reason, the "reserves" and the supply of raw materials and energy taken from the "reserves" can increase, even though the amount of "resources" constantly decreases. The physical scarcity of the "resources" in the deposits under the earth as such has no significance for the market. Thus, it seems that they are always in abundance, waiting only, so to speak, for exploration and exploitation.

It is also important that the exploitation can be accelerated without increasing marginal costs. Alfred Marshall was the first to call attention to this fact, when he noted:

> The supply of agricultural produce and of fish is a perennial stream; [but] mines are as it were Nature's reservoir. The more nearly a reservoir is exhausted, the greater is the labor of pumping from it; but if one man could pump it out in 10 days, ten men could pump it out in one day: and when once empty, it would yield no more. . . . If the plans had been properly laid in advance, and the requisite specialized capital and skill got ready for the work, 10 years' supply of coal might have been raised in one year without any increased difficulty. (Marshall 1890, p. 219)

Of course, after a deposit is exhausted, one has to change to another deposit, where the extraction costs may be higher, but this can, at least to a certain degree, be compensated with an increased use of machinery and a simultaneous expansion of production combined with technical progress, thus lowering the average costs. Only when deposits in the deep sea must be exploited, where the access to the site is extremely difficult, the increase of costs of exploitation will definitely prevail.

Certainly, in the end, earth's total supply of "resources" will have been explored and converted to "reserves," whose finiteness will also then become an economically relevant factor. But this is not imminent. The "resources" of raw materials in general are, with some exceptions, still extraordinarily large, augmented by the recycling of waste products.

Equally, energy "resources," as a whole, are likewise still by no means facing their ultimate exploitation, despite the fact that energy cannot be recycled, but rather dissipates in the atmosphere as waste heat. Although it is assumed that, at a constant rate of consumption, the extractible supplies of conventional oil will be exhausted in about 80–100 years, the total supply of biogenic energy sources, also at a constant rate of consumption, should still last many centuries.[4] But the drawback is their CO_2 emissions, which are the main cause of the climate change. Nevertheless, there are substitutes available. For a while nuclear energy was considered to be an "endless" source of energy, in the assumption that its nuclear waste (plutonium) could in turn be used as a new source of energy. But the dangers of this technology have made it controversial today. The direct or indirect use of solar energy is frequently propagated in its various forms, with references to the fact that the solar energy that radiates the earth per m^2 is about 1,000 times as much as the energy consumption per m^2 today, even when it has to be borne in mind that the land upon which the solar energy is captured is limited, because land must serve a multitude of purposes. Geothermal energy may become an important source of energy that can be extracted from deeper and deeper strata of the earth. New technologies are also on the horizon. Thus, there will be no actual shortage of energy in general, but the price of energy will increase, because all alternative to conventional oil are more costly and have different drawbacks.

Included among the natural resources are not only those that are involved in production through their active and passive functions but also those that have a *location function*. The "location" is to be understood here in a broader sense. It not only encompasses the land but also the sea and the air space.

Land is the world's scarcest resource. Beyond the direct, noneconomic demand for a living space for men, animals, and plants, it is subject to a wide variety of economic demands. In this respect, it particularly serves:

- As a basis for agrarian production
- As sites for buildings of all kinds, including infrastructure for transport, garbage dumps, and landfills
- As landscape claimed by the tourist industry
- As sites for producing renewable energies (primarily hydropower, photovoltaic, wind power, and biomass)
- As sites for accessing mineral resources for their exploitation.

[4] According to the World Energy Council, Report 1995, the proven reserves, plus the reserves of fossil biogenic energy sources at the threshold of being exploited, amount to 5,090 gigatons of oil equivalent (gtoe). In addition, estimates resources amount to 5,300 gtoe. If we assume that half of that is actually retrievable, we have a total amount of 7,740 gtoe. This is to compare with an annual consumption of 7.0 gtoe.

Between the economically exploited areas, there can still be found today a few areas of former "wilderness" that have, until now, escaped economic demand. However, these areas are constantly shrinking. For this reason, it is becoming increasingly more difficult to assert economic claims to land at the cost of the "wilderness." And so, quite apart from noneconomic demands, conflicts might arise between different economic demands for the use of the land, even when multipurpose utilization of the land is to a certain extent possible.

In principle, such conflicts are settled by the original claim to the land and the right of ownership. This makes it possible to trade land on the real estate market. In this trade, the use of land will prevail that promises the greatest financial gain per acre. This is predominantly the use for building houses and factories that is supported by the influx of goods and services from nonrenewable resources that do not need much land for extraction. In contrast to it, the use of land for farming, that is, using land as a renewable resource, needs a large amount of acres. For this reason alone, the financial gain per acre is here considerably less. Consequently, in a growing economy, there is extensive conversion of agricultural land, as well as of forests, steppes, and mountain, into building plots. Of course, infrastructure costs must be taken into account. But these incur only once and are relatively small.

But the market is not only decisive for the use of the land. The owner's rights to the land were and are complemented to a certain degree by laws, taxes, and subsidies of the state. On the one hand, there are measures to inhibit the conversion of land into building land, but on the other hand, there are measures to accelerate this conversion. The trend toward increasing conversions must prevail to support the growth process, although opportunity costs are incurred which are intentionally suppressed.

The sea is the second location resource, serving mainly for shipping of bulk goods. Its contribution to the steadily increasing net product and the economic growth is enormous. It was through maritime shipping that global trade and the international division of labor developed. Shipping of bulk goods began some 3,000 years ago in the Mediterranean. It was an invention of the Phoenicians. Its next big boom came when the Portuguese and Spanish sought a sea route to India and, in the process, discovered America at the close of the fifteenth century. This ushered in the modern era. But it was only since the industrial revolution that maritime shipping became, under the leadership of England, the very foundation of economic growth. It has remained so despite the increase in freight traffic on land and in the air.

Appropriation of the sea had not been necessary because there is almost no rivalry among the users. Since ancient times, seafaring nations have insisted on the freedom of the seas, meaning above all the capability of sailing through straits and the right to use harbors. This right was repeatedly contested and to some extent even suspended. Despite this, the sea has essentially remained "res nullius." It belongs to no one. That means its use, aside from landing charges, costs nothing.

This is similarly true for the third location resource: the air as space for air transportation. Its importance for the development of trade and, with it, of economic growth, is still increasing. But its expansion may be hindered by the necessity of regulating flight altitudes and directions due to the actual limits of the use of air as air space.

This overview of natural resources as the basis for economic growth shows the necessity to differentiate between the different types of resources. In general, it can be assumed that there is still a great potential for their use. Nevertheless, opportunity, restitution, or loss costs increase continuously. This will result in increasing conflicts of use and an increase in the prices of the resources.

6.3 Imagination as an Intellectual Resource

The human intellect or imagination is to the economy what sunlight is to the ecological cycle as a constantly self-regenerating driving force. Through the discovery and invention of new production processes and new products, it keeps competition alive and, with the help of competition, the market process. This is not a matter of increasing the productivity of labor or capital in abstracto, not a "deus ex machina," as conventional economics would assume. It is rather largely a matter of intensifying the exploitation of nature, expanding the use of materials and energy derived from nature.

Imagination, which is operative in all phases of production, provides a considerable contribution to the net product. It certainly also requires logistics: The living costs of the persons doing the research must be paid for, as well as the maintenance and operation of educational and research institutions that provide the means they need for the research. This incurs considerable restitution costs. But the value of these services is by far higher than the costs incurred.

Today it is not (any longer) left up to the market to decide whether the restitution costs will be covered or not. Instead, a major portion of the costs of education and research is assigned to the state, so that the human imagination can develop as much as possible.

Just as nature's integration into production, the integration of imagination is an ongoing process. Innovations emerge in this process partly as free goods, partly as intellectual property by the authors or by the companies that have purchased the intellectual property. Innovations may result in a patent that can be sold as such.

There is a detailed discussion in economic theory about the optimal form patent rights should take, particularly concerning the duration of patent protection. This is with the understanding that the patent right would tend to have a positive effect on the number of inventions and on their use (see Tirole 1997, 399ff.). Indeed, such an effect can be assumed because of the high costs that often are incurred for obtaining a patent.

In conventional economics, imagination is almost exclusively associated with the invention of new methods of production, hardly ever with the invention of new products. In reality, however, innovation has always, and especially since the industrial revolution, been characterized by the production of first thousands and then hundreds of thousands of different industrial products that satisfy new wants.[5]

This brings us back to the teachings of Georg Schlosser (see above p. 51f) and his differentiation between agricultural products and the "forms," that is, finished products "formed" from agricultural or other materials. Schlosser contradicts the point of view of the physiocrats that agricultural products command higher prices than the "forms," that is, the finished products of handicraft or industry. This idea was based on the fact that agricultural products are for the most part food and that these, being essential to life, meet a relatively inflexible demand. Schlosser showed that this argumentation was flawed. In particular, he pointed out that with "forms" goods are created for new wants and they can be sold at higher prices, depending on the intensity of these new wants. Through the fostering of new wants that the people receive from "new teachers and inventors," new forces are mobilized for production and "form shaping." In the language of conventional economics, this means that the traditional agricultural commodities are subject to the "law" of diminishing marginal utility or the "law" of saturation. As soon as the supply is large enough to satisfy the hunger, the demand for an increased amount of these goods is drastically reduced. In contrast, the new—in Schlosser's term, the refined—industrial goods have a higher marginal utility when they first come on the market. If the marginal utility of these new goods also falls when they are in greater supply, other goods appear on the horizon that once again have a higher marginal utility, etc. There is always a "hunger" for something new.

Nevertheless, new products must at least satisfy a latent genuine want. If not, no one will buy them. This can be seen in the many products that "died" shortly after being introduced to the market. Apparently, they did not meet any genuine want. This raises the question as to whether the reservoir of genuine wants has finite dimensions or whether imagination can invent new products in unending succession that can suffice genuine wants. Only then do they meet a repeatedly new and relatively inelastic demand that can enable a high rate of profits and, with help of the high rate of profits, a steady growth of the economy. Can imagination accomplish this? It is actually plausible to assume so because there is a huge reservoir of wants that are considered insatiable.

Belonging to the *first* category of insatiable or barely satiable wants are the wants for comfort, mobility, information, psychological well-being, and a long life.

Man wants to live effortlessly; in other words, he wants to avoid having to wipe the sweat off his brow with which he has been cursed since his banishment from paradise. He has come a long way already and he continues to progress further. This does not mean that he is not willing to exert himself; it just has to be voluntary

[5] The philosopher Leopold Ziegler speaks of the idiosyncrasy of mankind, "in constantly shifting the limits of his needs upward, virtually moving them into infinity, even though they are clearly drawn downward." In this manner, needs are being replaced by constantly expanding wants. Given this, Ziegler speaks of the modern economy as the "economy of wants" which has replaced the "economy of needs" (Ziegler 1927, p. 159).

and not out of necessity, only out of a creative mood, as a hobby, or as sport. Nevertheless, the necessity to work cannot be totally vanquished since man does have to eat each day. He must acquire the products that he needs by at least a minimum of labor. But the acquisition can always be made ever more and more effortlessly.

Man also strives for mobility. He wants to move quickly to be everywhere at once. He strives for ubiquity. This can never be completely attained since man is subject to temporal restrictions and it takes time to overcome each distance. But it is certainly possible to continually reduce the time needed to travel from one place to the next. Man can still become more mobile.

Although modern man knows a lot, he still wants to "know everything," as Wagner, Faust's assistant in Goethe's drama, says. So at least man is seeking to get informed as much as possible about the potential of available knowledge. This desire of man is being met by the computer and the internet, which provide him access to a great accumulation of knowledge without which he would have to go personally to a library or get some other source of information, which takes a lot of time. Although mankind will never have access to all information, and certainly not to all knowledge, it is possible to continually expand information options, to channel information more effectively and to make it still easier to access.

Psychological well-being can be increased furthermore by products that invite the consumer to active participation, especially by works of art that delight the beholder, reader, spectator, or listener, insofar as that person "has something to add to it," as Goethe says, but also by products that provide the consumer with a passive thrill, such as drugs of all kinds. To this can be added entertainment such as games, circuses, festivals, and Disneylands of all varieties that are half art and half drugs. The need for art, drugs, and entertainment is apparently insatiable because fantasy and addiction are always two steps ahead of their gratification.

Man can never come to terms with his own mortality. Therefore he is always searching for possibilities to prolong his life. This is where medicine and the pharmaceutical industry step in. There is supposed to be a remedy for every illness. Death is considered to be a failure of medicine. In reality man is destined to die because he was born as mortal. But it is nevertheless possible to cure or at least alleviate an increasing number of diseases and ailments with modern medicines and modern medical techniques, with death tending to be postponed ever further.

A *second* category of insatiable wants is the need for so-called status symbols, those products that are sought after because they distinguish the owner. This includes luxury goods of all kinds that have a value because not everyone can afford them, making them a mark of higher social status. Commonly this is referred to conspicuous consumption. When the ownership of these products becomes widespread, and those with a hitherto lower status move up, then new products must be found or invented that provide their owners once again with a higher status. The want for goods that enables such upward mobility in a growing economy is, by its own logic, never ending (see Hirsch 1995).

A *third* category of insatiable wants includes those whose insatiability is not inherent in themselves but rather develops out of the insufficient satisfaction of other needs. This results in a need for products that either correct or compensate for this insufficient satisfaction. We have pointed out that in utilizing nature external costs can incur. Therefore, devices of all kind are needed that serve to correct or to compensate them. These wants are in principle insatiable because in a growing economy there will be always new external costs and the devices that correct or compensate them may themselves cause new external costs.

The scope of imagination is, therefore, limitless, either because wants are in themselves unending, or because a want results from the dynamics of conspicuous consumption, or because the need for correction or compensation is an endless chain of external costs.[6]

However, it must be borne in mind that new products can force old products not only partially but completely off the market, for example, natural medicaments were replaced by chemical products. In this case, a loss of utility occurs for those who would have preferred to continue buying the traditional product. The fact that an ever-increasing amount of advertising is necessary to sell products to the consumers also clearly indicates that the number of new products is increasing faster than their acceptance by the consumer. A portion of income growth is then wasted on advertising costs.[7]

Despite this critique, it can be assumed that because of the steady increase in shopping space and sales shelves all over the world, the human imagination is at least capable of stopping the effect of the "law" of diminishing marginal utility, so that with increased production for the market, there will also still be an increase in the overall utility of production.

6.4 Conclusion

Our survey of natural resources and the possibility of their use leads to the conclusion that they do not enter the economic arena because of their scarcity but because of their abundance. Renewable resources can be included in the growth process primarily through more intensive cultivation of land, the increasing exploitation of nonrenewable resources, and the concentration on an even more profitable use of location resources.

However, compared to traditional agriculture, this does entail higher cultivation, access, exploration, and exploitation costs as part of the restitution costs.

[6] Ulrich Witt (2002) offers a similar explanation for a constantly growing economy. He assumes a category of elementary wants that are basically satiable. But these can build up into so-called combination goods, whose various elements are satisfied at different rates. In addition, the learned or conditioned wants build on the elementary wants, such as the want to collect paintings or other things and the want for goods with instrumental character, foremost the want for information.

[7] The compulsive character of always having to consume more and more can also be considered as a problem burdening the consumer because he is never allowed to be satisfied. Geminello Alvi sees consumers as virtual victims: "They are condemned to always consume more and more ... What they consume is irrelevant. It is only important ... to train the people for economic growth". (Alvi 1989, p. 64)

But despite this increase of the restitution costs, natural resources remain the fundament of the *net product* because, when nature is taken in possession and used, it demands nothing in return. This appropriation is a one-sided business deal. In principle it is free of charge.

The "law" of diminishing marginal returns has practically no meaning in the modern industrial economy where increasing returns are produced by machine- and energy-driven mass production.

The vast potential of natural resources has the effect that from an economic point of view only minor opportunity costs—primarily when dealing with land—and minor loss costs—primarily when dealing with water—are incurred, even if these costs are high from an ecological point of view. The result is that the economy does not focus on the efficient use of the resources, but is instead (still) able to concentrate first and foremost on using the available potential of natural resources and imagination for achieving economic growth.

Given these conditions, it is not adequate to view production in the modern economy as an optimization of the use of scarce resources as was the case in traditional agriculture and the Robinson Crusoe economy. The price of natural resources or their use does reflect only a transitory scarcity that can be continuously overcome by increasing the supply. It is dependent upon how quickly, how much, and at what cost the increase in supply is provided.

All in all, it can be assumed that there will be no immediate limits to growth, neither with regard to an absolute scarcity of resources nor with regard to a definitive saturation of wants. There will nevertheless be a shortage of resources that are easily accessible and a rivalry of different kinds of uses. This shortage or rivalry will impede growth but will not prohibit it for a foreseeable future.

Income Distribution in the Process of Growth

7

7.1 The Distribution of the Social Product on the Basis of the Net Product or Surplus Theory

In order to arrive at an adequate statement about the distribution of the social product in the growing economy, we must replace the marginal productivity theory by the net product or surplus theory. The essence of the net product or surplus theory is to distinguish between the restitution costs and the net product, that is, the amount by which the social product exceeds the restitution costs. Only the net product allows an enjoyment of goods that is an end in itself, not a mere necessity, and which therefore means riches in the truest sense of that word. The crucial thing in connection with economic growth and the distribution of the increasing social product is therefore that the increase in the product should exceed the increase in restitution costs.

According to the net product theory, restitution costs include not only the replacement investments but also the costs that are necessary to guarantee the subsistence minimum of the worker and his family as well as the maintenance of the natural bases of economic development. To a certain extent, it today includes also the maintenance of education and research, commensurate with the significance of the human imagination as another important production factor.

In addition, the net product theory also opens the possibility of incorporating the factor that dominates the modern economic system but plays no part in the "Robinson Crusoe" economy: the money capital as a factor of promotion. This factor makes a contribution to production without actually being itself physically involved in the production process. Capital is the money that the firms require in order to be able to prefinance production. Without capital, that is, without advanced money, there would be no firms, without firms no division of labor, and without division of labor it would not be possible to achieve such enormous increases in the social product as was possible since the industrial revolution.

Because capital as a factor of promotion is money, the increase in production triggered by the investment of capital can only be achieved by a consistent

H.C. Binswanger, *The Growth Spiral*, DOI 10.1007/978-3-642-31881-8_7,

monetization of the economy. This is necessary because firms pay the services of labor, nature, and imagination from money capital. Thus, all income—wages and rents—are a priori monetary incomes. This is of course also true for the income of the owners of the capital itself, that is, the net profit of the shareholders and the interest of the banks.[1]

The so-called "real" capital, that is, the sum of the produced means of production, that is, machinery and other equipments, is as such not involved in the distribution of income. The produced means of production are—as the term itself says—products themselves that are produced by the original factors of production: labor, nature, and imagination. The total income must be assigned to the original factors or rather to those who own them, in addition to money capital as a factor of promotion, that is, for the prefinancing of production that is necessary due to the fact that production precedes sales in time. This observation makes it possible to eliminate the construct "real" capital, that is, the produced means of production, from the catalog of income earners. This is a construct that found a place in the theory of distribution only because the static neoclassical theory had no use for the time structure of the production-sale process.

The firms are entitled to all the money that they earn in return by the sale of their products. This right is derived from the fact that they paid all the services that are necessary for the manufacturing of the products. What has been bought and paid belongs to the buyer! This means that the firms who pay the services may also keep for themselves any surplus that might be left over from the earnings after the expenses for the payment of the production services have been deducted.

The remuneration of the production factors, paid by the firms, is allocated to the owners of the factors according to the actual rights of ownership. This means that the distribution of income is not merely determined by the service of the factors but also by the institutional rules governing the distribution of property.

In the case of *labor*, the performer of the service and the recipient of the income are one and the same. Since the abolition of slavery, the worker is at the same time the owner of his manpower. It is to him that the remuneration for the work done accrues.

In the case of *nature,* the performer of the service and the recipient of the income are two totally separate entities. Nature performs a service for which the owner of nature does not have to pay anything. It can be a free good like air; then, it is a common property and has no price. But mostly nature has a private owner, who is entitled to demand on the market a price for the service of nature, called rent. The owner is, so to speak, regarded as the "producer" of this service and this regardless of whether he has worked on nature himself or employed others to do that for him.

The *products of imagination* have, so to speak, two "performers": on the one side, the human mind that can spark an idea in *anyone* and is therefore a common property

[1] Cf. also Erich Preiser (1961b, p. 269): "The demand [for the services of the factors of production] is not primary but derived. It is not the definitive consumer who is providing the demand according to his list of priorities, but the entrepreneur, who values the services in terms of their 'productivity' and otherwise orients himself to the goal of maximum profits."

of all men, and on the other side, the inventor, whose job it is to transform imagination into a tangible form and can claim a private property for his service. The question is, therefore, which of these is to be regarded as the *true* originator of the invention. The products of the human mind will be regarded as common property, if they are perceived as being above all a performance of the human mind. In this case, all may avail themselves of the product of the imagination. The inventor cannot in such a case demand any fee in return for his service. If, however the product of the imagination is regarded as a service provided by the inventor, the inventor will be entitled to receive a fee or a rent for the product. It is to this end that patent laws were created. The inventor is, with the patent given, the proprietor, who sells his invention. In practice we have a mixture of both concepts. The right of ownership, which the investor derives from the patent laws, is only granted under certain conditions and always only for a limited period of time. Thus, the concept that the imagination/human mind is common property still has a certain validity. The same is true for the property rights of the authors of books derived from the copyright law.

The owners of the *capital of the firm* are the shareholders in the case of equity capital, that is, the households who own shares, and in the case of borrowed capital the banks or rather the shareholders of the banks—the households again. The profit of the firm is attributed to the capital of the firm, which has to pay a part of it in the form of interest to the bank and another part in the form of dividends to the shareholders of the firm. But a part of the profit is retained by the firm. The shareholders participate also in the retained profit in the form of an increase in the values of their shares since the firm reinvests the retained profits. The reinvestment of the profits contributes to the future increase in profits and in this way also to the increase of the dividends.

This overview of the different factors influencing the distribution of income in a growing economy shows that the marginal productivity theory—apart from its inherent deficiencies—cannot constitute a valid distribution theory for the modern economy. If we put the net product theory in its place, the distribution theory may indeed lose some of its elegance, but it also gains not only a significantly greater degree of realism but also the ability to analyze the various determining factors in the historical context.

If we use the net product or surplus theory and start out from the physiocratic, the mercantilist, and the classical tradition, we have the possibility of explaining the distribution of income in the light of the development of the last centuries. This explanation is based on the relation between the net product and the restitution costs and the distribution of the net product.

In the physiocratic situation on which Quesnay based his model, the restitution costs are to be found in that part of the total product which must remain in the hands of the producers—the farmers—in order that their subsistence is guaranteed. This includes also the share of the annual production which is required for the maintenance of the buildings and the equipment. The land regenerates itself, which means that the restitution costs for the land are zero. Neither will any additional access costs be incurred in terms of clearing, as the physiocrats assumed that all available fertile space has already been put under the plow. The imagination has no place of its own in Quesnay's physiocratic theory and does not, therefore, contribute anything to the surplus. Thus, the total net product or surplus depends on the fertility of the cultivated land.

The production process is performed within the annual cycle of sowing and harvesting. There is no need for any capital as a factor of promotion. In this situation, the entire income is divided between labor and land, in this case between the farmers and the landlords. But the question is whether the farmer gets only an income in the amount of the restitution costs or also receives a share of the net product or surplus. The physiocrats deny that. They based their theory upon the situation in France during the eighteenth century. The surplus belongs, according to the laws of ownership, exclusively to the landlords, who demand it as a rent from the farmers, their traditional tenants. In other countries and at other periods of time—as the physiocrats were aware—it is nevertheless possible that the land belong to the farmers themselves. In this case, the farmers receive the rent from the land which belongs to them. The decisive factor for the allocation of the surplus is therefore the law of land ownership.

The physiocrats tacitly assume that the competition in manufacturing is so great that the manufacturers, with the prices which they receive for their products, can just get the bare minimum—the restitution costs—necessary for their survival.

According to the physiocrats' view, therefore, the distribution of income is above all dependent on the regulation of ownership and the competitive situation amongst the suppliers.

In the mercantilistic and even more so in the classical situation, both the agricultural and the industrial sectors have already been structured according to the principle of division of labor. Capital plays already an important role as a factor of promotion. Therefore, the situation in England in the seventeenth and eighteenth, and most particularly in the nineteenth centuries, differs significantly from that of France during the eighteenth century. In the English situation, there are not only two but three types of income recipients: the landowners, the laborers, and the capitalists. In the following, we will describe in detail the circumstances prevailing in the nineteenth century as Ricardo saw them.

Ricardo regards labor as the sole production factor, even though he does also speak of the "indestructible powers" of the land. But it is this very "indestructibility" that prevents him from regarding land as a production factor, because in his view, a factor is only a production factor if he receives income to cover restitution costs. But the land regenerates itself. Thus, it does not require restitution costs in the same way as labor does. Therefore, the landowners are not entitled to demand payment for the productive services provided by the land. For this reason Ricardo—contrary to the physiocrats—does not regard land as a production factor. The landlord is in his eyes merely a beneficiary who does not actually do anything in return for what he receives.

The value of the produced means of production—the so-called "real" capital—has according to Ricardo to be ascribed to the labor costs. No specific form of income can therefore be attributed to them, neither as rents nor as profits nor as interests.

Yet, in a similar way as did the physiocrats, Ricardo also assumes that the laborers earn more or less only the minimum required for their existence, so that their income may therefore increase a little but only a little above the level of the subsistence wage.

In England agriculture was organized along capitalistic lines. The capitalists—these were the leaseholders who advanced the capital and have practiced agriculture as a firm—sell the products that are made by the laborers with the aid of the produced means of production and the contributions of the land. They pay the laborers a part of the proceeds in the form of wages according to the terms of the labor contract. The wages are subject to the constant pressure of competition on the labor market as there are more laborers available than are required by the agricultural and industrial sectors. That explains why the laborers had to be content more or less with the subsistence wage.

Thus, the net product or surplus is according to Ricardo divided, in both the agricultural and industrial sector, by the landlords and the capitalists according to the laws of ownership. The capitalists own the produced means of production but not the land, which they lease from the landlords. They pay a rent to them. The remaining part of the surplus is retained by the capitalists as profits, to which they lay claim in return for the advance of money performed by the capital invested.

New productions methods or new products are only mentioned in passing by Ricardo. They do not have a central role to play. As a consequence, there is no room in his distribution theory for the service of imagination and rents paid for their services.

The Ricardian distribution theory is lent its true flavor by the dynamism which—according to Ricardo—results in the gradual redistribution of incomes from the capitalists to the landlords. This is triggered by the increase of population and the resultant increase in the demand for food. The increase of population is made possible by the fact that the wages exceed, if only by a little, the subsistence wage so that more children can be fed than would be necessary merely to replace their parents. Consequently, an ever-increasing amount of less suitable land must be cultivated. This causes the costs of food production on marginal land to increase and with them the prices for the foodstuffs, as these must cover the higher costs of production on the marginal land. The higher prices also apply to those quantities that are produced on land of a better quality. Owing to these higher prices for agricultural products, the laborers in turn also require higher wages in order to guarantee their own existence or, to put it another way, to cover the restitution costs of their labor. At the same time, the rents received by the owners of the land and with them the share of rents in the surplus also increase. The gain of the capitalists is thus "sandwiched" between these two sides, higher wages (because of higher restitution costs) and higher rents. The profits become less and less. When it reaches zero, no new capital is formed, and the economy will cease to grow. The economy will return to the situation as it was described by the physiocratic theory. The entire surplus will then belong to the landlords. Ricardian dynamism is thus a form of dynamism that brings itself to a standstill.

The classic distribution theory in Ricardo's sense is based, like that of the physiocrats, on the assumption that the distribution of income is dependent upon both the ownership rights and the competitive situation. Ricardo, however, added the historical development induced by the growth process itself as an essential co-determining factor.

The distribution of income in the industrial countries developed however in a totally different manner than had been assumed by Ricardo. The share of rents in the national income decreased, whilst those of wages and profits increased. The modern dynamism is not one that brings itself to a standstill but rather one that reinforces itself.

Today, restitution costs for the provision of natural services have to be accepted where previously none have been incurred. This is the price to be paid for their ever more intensive use. Such costs are the result of the necessity of maintaining the proceeds from agriculture through the use of fertilizers, pesticides, etc., as well as the necessity of replenishing the supplies of nonrenewable resources by constant exploration and the necessity of conserving nonagricultural renewable resources—forestry, grazing, fishing, exploitation of wild plants, and animals—by maintenance measures of all kinds.

The consequence is not, however, that the prices for the services provided by nature—foodstuffs, raw material, and energy—would have increased accordingly, because all these products are homogeneous goods and are therefore subject to strong price competition. Therefore, they are able to achieve only low prices. The only possibility to increase profits is to increase the amount of production. Accordingly the prices of these products and with it the profits attained by the sale of them remain relatively low.

Competition is particularly intensive with regard to the agricultural products that millions of farmers bring onto the market. As a result of the pressure on prices exerted by semi-industrial farms that produce on large areas of land with the aid of industrially produced means of production, the land rent of the majority of the traditional agricultural farms—the so-called family farms—would sink to zero or even less than zero. They are therefore only able to survive thanks to the support—granted in a variety of ways—by the agricultural policy of the state that at least covers the restitution costs.

Greater profits can be made from the exploitation of mineral and energy resources as the competition among the mining firms is restricted on the one hand by the fact that the state only grants a certain number of concessions in return for concession fees or royalties and on the other hand by the significant amount of capital required that only very large firms have at their disposal. Nevertheless, as the raw materials and energy are also goods of a homogeneous nature and therefore subject to intensive price competition, the possibilities for price increases depend on the possibility of cartelization. But cartelization is always a fragile construction.

To summarize, the surpluses that arise from large scale use of the natural resources do not primarily lead to rent building but are passed on either to the producers of the final goods or, if the competition of these producer is strong enough, to the consumers of the final goods.

The products of imagination can be taken into ownership only to a limited extent, notwithstanding an extension of patent or copyright protection. The rents for imaginative services therefore make also only a modest contribution to the national income.

The most important change for the distribution of the national income since the beginning of the industrial revolution was the relative new scarcity of labor in the industrialized countries. This has enabled the workers to obtain wages that were well in excess of the restitution costs. Real wages have furthermore increased disproportionately because the prices for the basic products, in particular foodstuffs, have lagged behind. In consequence the costs of the average household on food and other goods required to meet a person's basic needs only account for a small proportion of the total budget of the average household. This effect was described in the middle of the nineteenth century by the Saxon statistician Ernst Engel in "Engel's Law."[2]

The low level of wages in the industrialized world at the beginning of the nineteenth century had been due, in addition to the increase in population, to the emigration from the countryside. This emigration arose because the competition from the factories destroyed the cottage industry, which provided the agricultural sector a subsidiary source of income, and because the agricultural sector itself required less labor as a consequence of the increased productivity of the agriculture thanks to the new cultivation and fertilization methods.

Towards the end of the nineteenth century, however, the increase in population slowed down. Furthermore, the industrial economy grew and with it the demand for labor. In such a situation, it was possible for the trade unions, founded in the course of the nineteenth century, to enforce additional restrictions in the labor market resulting not only in higher wages but also in restrictions upon working hours, which made labor even more scarce and led in turn to further wage increases.

Nevertheless, the substitution of labor by energy—formerly mainly by the mechanization of manufacturing processes, today primarily as a result of the computerization of industrial and office operations—has kept and will continue to keep increases in wages in check to a certain degree. This leaves enough room for profits and prevents wages from "winning" against profits.

The capital incorporated in a firm is the primary recipient of earnings in the economy. The firms are entitled to retain all earnings, inasmuch as these do not have to be passed on in the form of wages due to the laborer, rents due to the owners

---

[2] Engel's Law states: "A poor person may indeed spend a lower amount of money on the necessities of life than a prosperous one, but nonetheless a larger percentage of his income. The higher a person's income, the larger the percentage that remains for less urgent expenses" (Ernst Engel 1857). Engel's Law has subsequently been broadened by the inclusion of all goods essential to life. This extended version was first put into words by Julius Faucher in two essays on "Currency and Prices" (1868/9). Cf. Rieter (2002, 35f). He emphasizes that Faucher "[identifies] the path of the transmission of monetary impulses to cash value not in the effect of the *level* of demand and prices (as did later the disciples of Keynes, for example) but in their effect upon the *structure* of those variables" (2002, p. 38).

of land and other natural resources or for services of imagination. If the rents lag behind and the wages are kept within certain limits, then the lion's share of the increasing surpluses "sticks" to the capital of the firm.

Under these circumstances, the profit rate—that is, the firm's profit in relation to the firm's total capital—increases. The same is true for the return on equity, that is, the relation between net profit and equity capital, because the interest rate remains at a relatively low level. This results from the ability of the banking sector to provide credits without definitive limits on the basis of money creation.

Adam Smith described the ideas concerning net profits as follows: "Double interest is in Great Britain reckoned, what the merchants call, a good, moderate, reasonable [net] profit; terms which I apprehend mean no more than a common and usual [net] profit" (Smith 1976, Bk 1, Ch. IX, 168). As the interest rate, according to his figures, was 4–5 % for good debtors, this meant that, in those days, the usual rate of [net] profits was ca. 8–10 %.

After interest levels had fallen in the course of the nineteenth and twentieth century to ca. 3–4 % today's [net] profit expectations are higher. These must be estimated at 2–3 times the rate of interest, that is, ca. 10–15 %. These expectations are being fulfilled to a large extent, even though they do, of course, depend upon the outcome of the market processes and cannot therefore be guaranteed.

If we regard the development of wages and profits during the twentieth century, we see that the antagonism between them has, in the longer run, turned into a symbiosis. This results from the fact that the firms can only sell their increasing production on the market when the wages also increase, thus leading to a higher demand. Reciprocally the households may only then expect wages to increase if higher profit expectations lead to increasing demand for labor.

This recognition has led to the compromise that has been decisive for the development of the distribution of profits and wages during the twentieth century, namely, the rule that wages should increase in accordance with the increase in productivity. The prerequisite for this, however, is the constant increase in the surplus of the national income in excess of the restitution costs of labor.

But the basic tendency in the symbiotic development of wages and profits is being modified in the twenty-first century by globalization, so that the labor forces from the developing countries, which have considerably lower wages, are influencing the wage level of the industrialized countries. Thus, labor in the industrialized countries, in addition to the competition from energy, is facing further competition from labor from the developing countries.

The low level of wages in these countries is due to less capital being available per worker, the growth in population and the acceleration of the exodus from the rural areas to the cities, and thus to the intensification of the competition among the workers in the cities.

Yet, the new tendency towards a relative (!) reduction in wages in the industrialized countries is compensated to a certain extent by the fact that the households purchase shares and thus can participate in increasing profits. This participation comes primarily not from dividends but of the increase in the share prices achieved by the very fact that the largest part of the profits is *not* paid out as a dividend but retained within the firm; it is used, in other words, to refinance investments and thus increase profits in the future.[3] This possibility is essentially enhanced by the privatization of firms that had previously been in public ownership and the "going public" of private firms.

Adam Smith writes concerning the development of wages, profits, and rents: "In every society ... there is an ordinary or average rate both of wages and profit ... Likewise [there is also] in every society an ordinary or average rate of rent ... These ordinary or average rates may be called the natural wages, profit, and rent, at the time and place in which they commonly prevail" (Smith 1976, Bk 1, Ch. VII, 62). From the "natural prices" for the factors of production, calculated per production unit, the "natural price" of the commodity can be determined: "When the price of any commodity is neither more nor less than what is sufficient to pay the rent of the land, the wages of the labor, and the profits of the stock employed in raising, preparing, and bringing it to market, according to their natural rates, the commodity is then sold for what may be called its natural price." In the first part of our book, we described the "natural price" as the *reproduction price,* that is, that price that must at the very least realized on the market in order to cover the reproduction costs. This is the prerequisite for continued production, or reproduction. It may be stated once again: The reproduction costs include not simply the payments for the factors of production but also, viewed on a long-term basis, the payment for money capital as a factor of promotion.

By supplementing the concept of the *restitution costs* and the net *product or surplus* with the concept of *reproduction costs,* we may summarize the present distribution of national income or net social product, as it developed since the "classical situation" with the aid of these three terms as follows.

For services provided by *nature*, the owners can scarcely demand a reproduction remuneration in the form of a rent that is significantly above their restitution costs as the services of nature are constantly being increased. The share of the rent in the surplus therefore declines. The owners of the natural services—with the exception of the owners of energy resources—could therefore for the next future hardly expect that the growing contribution made by the services of nature to the national income will benefit them to a corresponding degree.

The owners of the services of imagination are also able to assert their claims only to a limited extent. The extent to which this may nonetheless prove possible depends upon the individual circumstances. Higher rents in individual cases are not ruled out.

In the energy sector, a "normal" or "natural" reproduction remuneration is impossible to identify. The price for the most important resource, oil, is in any event well above that of its reproduction price. A first increase was the consequence of the

[3] It has been empirically proven that, viewed on a long-term basis, investments in shares are on the whole more worthwhile than ones in bonds. This can be seen when one takes a look at the real average yield from shares in the period 1802–1998. This amounted to 7 % (cf. Jeremy J. Siegel 2000).

OPEC cartel in the 1970s. Since then, however, the price fell again. The resultant reluctance to expand production capacities or refineries on the one hand and the increased demand as a consequence of rapid economic growth in the developing countries on the other caused prices to rise again at the beginning of the twenty-first century leading to a further massive increase in excess of the restitution costs. In view of the probable continued increase in demand, it may be expected that, despite a new expansion of the supply, the price will remain high and will have a tendency to increase further. The acceleration in prices may nevertheless be expected to remain within certain limits as other sources of energy become available.

Wages, to which the households believe they are entitled, that is, the reproduction remuneration for *labor*, have increased in the industrialized world to a level well above the restitution costs for labor. It is therefore no longer simply a question of guaranteeing the subsistence minimum or survival of the worker and his family but also of enabling him to have a fair livelihood that includes the ability to gratify other needs that would formerly have been regarded as luxury wants. The workers or salaried employees are able today to assert these increased claims—in part with the aid of social legislation—as capital profits may only be increased if luxury consumption becomes mass consumption so that the employers are forced to permit significant increases in wages in order to be able to sell their products.

As Adam Smith recognized, the profit that the *capital* invested in the firm expects to achieve as a minimum is a part of the firm's reproduction costs. The capital invested in the firm demands such a "normal" remuneration in order to remain committed to the firm concerned and not "disembark" from it, in other words, in order that production might continue. This remuneration is, as we have already seen, increasing on the whole.

These findings may be summarized here in an overview, whereby we designate the restitution costs of the individual factors as c, the net product or surplus with s, the reproduction remuneration or "normal" or "natural" price with p^r, and the market price with p (whereby the "price for capital" is to be understood as the "remuneration" of the firm in form of profit). We use the suffixes:

n for nature
l for labor
k for capital

and for a small difference the symbol "$<$", for a larger one "$<<$" and for a very large one "$<<<$".

As a general rule, this means that:

- For nature (with the exception of energy) and similarly for imagination

$$p_n \approx p_n^r, p_n^r > c_n, s_n > 0$$

- For labor

$$p_l > p_l^r, p_l^r \gg c_l, s_l \gg 0$$

- For capital

$$p_k > p_k^r, p_k^r >>> c_k, s_k >>> 0$$

For the price of energy and in particular the amount by which that price exceeds the restitution costs, an upward trend can be identified. The increase in prices will, however, be counterbalanced by the availability of new energy resources.

In this connection, it should be pointed out once again that the price of the produced means of production can be broken down into the three components: rents, wages, and profits.

7.2 From the Nominal Social Product to the Effective Social Product: Amount and Distribution

So far we have dealt with the distribution of the social product as it is calculated in the official statistics. This includes only goods and services that are involved in monetary transactions. They are valued with their monetary prices. Therefore, the social product is a monetary quantity. It remains so, even if a price index is constructed, with which the increase in the nominal social product is discounted to get a so-called "real" social product. But this term is misleading in several respects. In order to obtain more information about of the goods and services that are indeed available for the satisfying of people's wants, we have to revise the concept of the nominal social product also in a number of other aspects. The result of such revisions will be called here the *effective social product*. These are, to a large extent, merely hypothetical revisions, as the corresponding figures cannot be procured, either for practical reasons or for reasons of principle. It is nevertheless important that such differences and their dimensions are ascertained.

In particular we must take into account that an ever-increasing number of goods and services, which before were produced by the consumer himself on the basis of self-sufficiency without any money involved, are now purchased on the market and paid with money. Although this is only a substitution process, for instance, substitution of cooking at home by eating in a restaurant, it appears in the official statistics as an increase of the "real" social product. But is not an increase in the effective social product.

The same applies to the products of nature that previously did not have to be paid for but which are successively being introduced into the market economy. For example, drinking water from the well is being increasingly replaced by bottled water. Or outdoor activities of different kinds are becoming products of the tourist industry. All these services previously "offered" by nature free of charge now cost money and are therefore wholly or partially declared as an increase in the so-called "real" social product, even though this increase is not a true one in the sense of the effective social product.

In order to arrive at the effective social product and thus avoid confusing substitution processes with genuine increases in production, the so-called "real" social product should first of all be extended to include the dimension of self-sufficiency and the priceless supplies of nature. Mere substitution processes would then appear with both a plus and a minus sign and therefore not as a net increase of the social product.

In an additional step, the difference between the so-called "real" social product and the effective social product must be established by including positive or negative side effects—the so-called external effects—of the economic production. The historically most significant positive side effect of economic production was the establishing of the cultivated landscape in connection with the gradual development of agriculture. But today, it is the negative side effects of accelerated growth of production on the environment that are at the focus of attention. They need to be perceived in the effective social product and thus accepted as loss costs.

7.3 Conclusion

Since the Industrial Revolution, that is, since the actual beginning of the growth process, the distribution of income has undergone considerable change. This is to a large extent a consequence of the growth process itself, that is, endogenous to it. From this it must be concluded that there cannot be any definitive rules pertaining to the distribution of incomes valid for all times as the marginal productivity theory would suggest. Instead of searching for such a general rule, one has therefore to ask whether the growth of the social product guarantees to the factors involved a net product, that is, a surplus in addition to the restitution costs. The true yield of the growth process is the increase of the surplus, not the increase of the restitution costs!

If we take a look at the development of wages since the beginning of the Industrial Revolution, we recognize that, in the beginning, these were only slightly higher than the restitution costs required to maintain the laborer and his family but have since then increased step by step, particularly since the middle of the twentieth century, to a level well above that, while the size of the labor-force or the working hours has hardly increased at all. Today, labor is able to claim a significant share of the net product or surplus.

This can be explained by the fact that the amount of services provided by the other factors, by nature and imagination, has multiplied to a huge extent, without a corresponding increase in their rents. The reason for this is that the products of nature and the imagination are available to their owners free of charge and, for the time being, only a small amount of restitution must be paid.

The capital as a factor of promotion requires only a modest amount of restitution costs as credits can be always expanded by money creation. It can be constantly increased at a low price, that is, at a (more or less) stable rate of interest determined by the central bank. The profit rate continues to depend to a certain extent upon the interest rate, even if the difference between the profit rate and the interest rate has grown larger till today.

The statements made so far apply essentially only to the industrialized world where capital has been able to unfold itself fully. Wages in the developing countries are lagging behind. They are nevertheless gradually on the increase, starting with those areas into which the availability of capital expands with the banking sector.

The increase in the income of labor, of the owner of nature and imagination, and of the owner of capital goes hand in hand with the increase in purchasing power but also with an increase of loss costs both in the area of production and of consumption. The difference between the "real" social product and the effective social product becomes larger and larger.

Part III

Money and Production in the Dynamics of the Growth Spiral: Growth Imperative and Growth Impetus

8 From the Theory of Growth to the Theory of the Growing Economy

The sustained growth process that began after the end of the Second World War made it necessary to add to the static neoclassical theory a separate theory of growth. The latter was established by R. M. Solow (1956) in his essay "A Contribution to the Theory of Economic Growth."

The attempt to integrate the phenomenon of economic growth in the conventional theory was additionally motivated by the development of a theory of growth within the post-Keynesian school, based on the work of Roy F. Harrod (1939) and E. D. Domar (1946). The starting point for the post-Keynesian theory of growth is Keynes' employment theory. Keynes had developed his "general theory" under the assumption that there would be a tendency to underemployment and, as a consequence, an underutilization of existing production capacities. He focused his entire attention upon increasing demand, since he assumed that an economic depression would result if the saving or hoarding of a portion of the national income was not counterbalanced by investments. He thereby overlooked the fact that investments do not only have an impact on incomes and therefore on demand but also on the production, as, due to the investments, "real" capital—mainly machines—also increases. This in turn led, as was emphasised by the post-Keynesian theory, to the danger of a constant underutilization of production capacity. The conclusion was that it is not sufficient to simply maintain the balance between saving and investing in order to maintain sufficient demand. It must also be assured that the income effect of investments on demand and the production (capacity) effect of investments on supply harmonize. But how is this to be achieved? According to the post-Keynesian theory of growth, it is achieved through further growth of investments by taking into account the time lag between the income and the production (capacity) effect of investments. The income effect makes itself felt immediately, that is, at the very moment when investments are made. The production effect, however, takes more time to manifest itself as the machines must first be manufactured and installed before the production of goods can be increased. This time lag makes it possible for the increased demand, which has been created by the growth of investments, to absorb the increased supply produced by investments made in the *previous period,* whilst the potential supply that is created *today* by the investments only comes on to the market *tomorrow*. This process can be continued ad infinitum if the rate of growth is just sufficient to bring the increased demand induced by the income effect of the present investment into harmony with the increased supply resulting from the production effect induced by the last investment. Such a balanced rate of growth, however, is not guaranteed. Balanced growth is therefore "knife edge" growth. From this it may be concluded that it is the duty of the state to maintain balanced growth, especially by promoting the demand side.

In contrast to this, the concern of the conventional theory of growth was to demonstrate that the market process *itself* tends to a balanced growth and, if any, only a supplementary support from the state—primarily on the supply side—is required.

The conventional theory of growth is based on the neoclassical Robinson Crusoe model, as was described in Chap. 2. It assumes a homogeneous production function in which only labor and capital are responsible for the creation of the social product. It is a theory in which money has no effect on real production. Capital is to be understood as "real" capital, that is, as the sum of the produced means of production (machines and other equipments) that are increased by investments. The investments are determined by savings. Labor and "real" capital are considered to be production factors that, to a large extent, can be substituted by each other. But the additional yield from a production factor decreases if the input of the other production factor either does not increase at all or only increases at a slower pace. The validity of the "law" of diminishing marginal return is thus presumed. As a general rule, constant returns of scale are presupposed, that is, the idea that output is doubled when the input of *both* production factors doubles.

Under these assumptions equilibrium of demand and supply together with full employment is always assured, but sustained growth of the social product is not possible without the help of a third factor. In view of the historical fact that labor, measured according to the size of the population, grew slower than "real" capital (which, admittedly, is difficult to measure), the growth of the social product would have to slow down. As this has not been the case, a factor that could fill the gap needed to be found. For this, Solow proposed "technical progress" that increases the effectiveness of labor from year to year. "Technical progress"—this is the decisive point—is not subject to diminishing marginal return.

However, this explanation of a constant rate of growth of the social product due to "technological progress" is a mere tautology. It falls like manna from heaven and is essentially unexplained. It is simply *assumed* that "technical progress" fills the gap that emerges due to the missing increase in the population and the resulting diminishing marginal return on capital. In his textbook "Advanced Macroeconomics," David Romer therefore speaks of a "mysterious variable, the 'effectiveness of labor,' whose exact meaning is not specified and where behaviour is taken as exogenous" (David Romer 1996, p. 95). He declares: "It is only a small exaggeration to say that we have been modelling growth by assuming it" (David Romer 1996, p. 25).

As a reaction to this situation, attempts were made to come up with a so-called endogenous theory of growth that would explain why the "law" of diminishing marginal return on capital is nullified in the growth process and why thus constant returns on capital may be assumed.[1]

We may reduce the various versions of an endogenous theory of growth to essentially four approaches. The first approach is the idea that the diminishing marginal return on capital is nullified by the fact that various forms of economic activity display positive external effects that are known as "spillovers"; this reflects the effects of "learning by doing." Second, we have to take into account the effects of inventions and information which, after a certain period of time, are available to everyone and third the effects of agglomeration benefits in so-called clusters. These positive effects can strengthen each other in the course of time.

The fourth approach is the conversion of labor to "human capital" that is seen as part of "real" capital. The result of this conversion is that only one production factor is left over, namely, "real" capital, into which human capital is incorporated. It is supposed that "human capital" can be constantly increased in terms of its effectiveness by investments in teaching and research.

All these approaches to an endogenous growth theory are certainly valuable, but are not sufficient to explain why the marginal return on capital remains exactly constant when growth in population lags behind. Solow draws attention to this himself. In his essay on "Perspectives in Growth Theory," he writes: "Now I return to the question of constant returns to capital. It may not be generally recognised how restrictive this assumption is. There is no tolerance for deviation. Lucas emphasised in his 1988 article, that a touch of diminishing returns to capital (human capital in this case) would change the character of the model drastically, making it incapable of generating growth. He did not notice that a touch of increasing returns to capital would do the same, but in a quite different way... It is obvious on the fact that there is potential for fairly explosive behaviour. ... The time path for this growth model has the property that the stock of capitals becomes infinite in finite time. It takes a little calculus to show that 'fairly explosive' puts it mildly" (Solow 1994, p. 50).

Solow sees at most a positive contribution of the theory of endogenous growth in the identification of endogenous components of technological progress. He insists however—correctly so—that there is an exogenous moment in the process of inventing new production technologies that is based on intuition or luck. This, however, means nothing else than that the endogenous theory of growth is not capable of fulfilling its own promises. It does not explain any better than did Solow's original theory, why the factors that it introduces should be able to adequately explain the historically observed steady increase in the social product, that is, to fill exactly the gap between the actual growth of the social product and the much smaller growth of the social product theoretically possible according to the neoclassical theory.

[1] The basis for this theory is formed by the essays written by Paul Romer (1986, 1990) and by Robert Lucas (1988). For an overview of the endogenous theories of growth cf. Lucas Bretschger (1996). A detailed analysis of the endogenous growth theory and corresponding statistical analyses may be found in Barro and Sala-i-Martin (1995).

Moreover, as formulated by Gene Grossman and Elhanan Helpman (1994), the justification of the theory of endogenous growth is obtained at the price of assumptions that contradict those of the neoclassical theory and raise doubts about the efficiency of markets, which this theory was meant to explain: "When growth is driven by endogenous innovation, two obstacles stand in the way of market efficiency. First, efficiency dictates marginal cost pricing [achieved by competition], but innovation requires the existence of monopoly profits. Second, efficiency demands that investment returns be fully appropriable, but the characteristics of knowledge suggest that spillovers [which are accessible to all men] will be prevalent" (Grossman and Helpman 1994, p. 37).

In addition, if by the inclusion of labor as "human capital" into capital the number of production factors is reduced to just a single one, the marginal productivity theory of distribution is implicitly abandoned, because it is no longer possible to explain the distribution of income between labor and capital on the basis of their respective marginal products. In this way, the raison d'être of the neoclassical theory is called into question. In fact, the purpose of neoclassical theory has been to demonstrate that the market mechanism leads to an efficient employment of the production factors under the condition of a general equilibrium in all relevant markets, in which the production factors are rewarded according to their marginal returns thanks to the effect of perfect competition. If there is only one production factor, a marginal return of a factor cannot be established. Therefore, we have to conclude that the so-called endogenous theory of growth cannot integrate the phenomenon of growth into neoclassical theory. Rather, it renders this theory invalid in its essential parts.

Therefore, we have to look for a new approach for the explanation of economic growth.

Such an approach is the economy theory presented here based upon the growth spiral. It provides an explanation of the modern economy as a phenomenon that, intrinsically, manifests itself as a growth process. The specific theory of growth is replaced by a general theory of the growing economy. This new theory is characterized by the following facts:

- The modern economy is a monetary economy in which firms need to have money capital at their disposal in order to be able to take up and continue their production activities and in which the deployment of capital must lead to a profit that justifies its deployment.
- Thanks to the creation of money, the deployment of capital can constantly be increased.
- Through the deployment of capital, the exploitation and utilization of natural resources are constantly intensified.
- There is an ever-increasing use of energy services that substitute and supplement labor.
- The performance of imagination is promoted by investments in research and development.

It can be assumed that human beings have a naturally induced desire for a "more" of goods. But the desire for an "*ever* more and more" can be better explained by the role of money in the modern economy.[2]

[2] Compared to similar observations made by Jürgen Löwe (1995, p. 91) about the "insatiable man": "A process of orienting human endeavour towards material objects must have taken place through the development of the western culture. With this, man, torn from his originally natural, religious and social integration, has tended to fall back more and more upon himself so that he no longer regards himself as an agent within a whole, but judges everything according to whether it corresponds to his own interests. The elements of the outside world, degraded to mere objects of possession, have become what man desires for himself. The right of ownership, created by man, guarantees the continued subordination of the object to the almost unrestricted power of the subject. Man's boundless desire for the acquisition of material goods as a result of cultural influences found ... in the institution of money an appropriately increasable good thanks to which his boundless desire could be realised."

9 The Economic Process as a Growth Spiral

The growing economy can be explained by an open-ended upward-going spiral of flows of goods and services and the corresponding monetary flows between firms and households. The spiral model differs from the circular flow model by the expansion of the economic process from period to period (cf. Fig. 9.1). This expansion results from an increase in the capital of firms, that is, by investments in connection with an increase in the size and the number of firms ($F_1 \rightarrow F_2 \rightarrow F_3 \rightarrow$), an increase in the income of households in connection with an increase in the number of households ($H_1 \rightarrow H_2 \rightarrow H_3 \rightarrow$), as well as—and this is the decisive factor—an increase in the amount of credit (loans) and money in connection with the increase of the banking system ($B_1 \rightarrow B_2 \rightarrow B_3 \rightarrow$). This occurs on the basis of an increasing use of nature and an increasing contribution by the imagination of the human mind, that is, of product and process inventions. The households provide the firms with their labor and other services. In return, they receive income from the firms in the form of wages, rents, and dividends. With this income they buy the products from the firms. To simplify the model, we neglect the government sector.

In our model all payments are effected via the banking system by bank money (we ignore payment with coins and bank notes). The monetary flow between firms and households encompasses wages, rents, dividends, and interest, paid by firms to households on the one side, and payments for products and also for shares and bonds issued by the firms, paid by households to firms on the other side. Additionally, there are payments between firms and between households.

In the diagram the circular flows are represented by thin arrows. The solid arrows represent the main characteristics of the growth model, namely:

- The creation of money initiated by new bank credits
- The increasing inflow of the services of nature (with an increasing outflow of waste and emissions to nature)
- An increasing inflow of the services of human imagination.

H.C. Binswanger, *The Growth Spiral*, DOI 10.1007/978-3-642-31881-8_9,

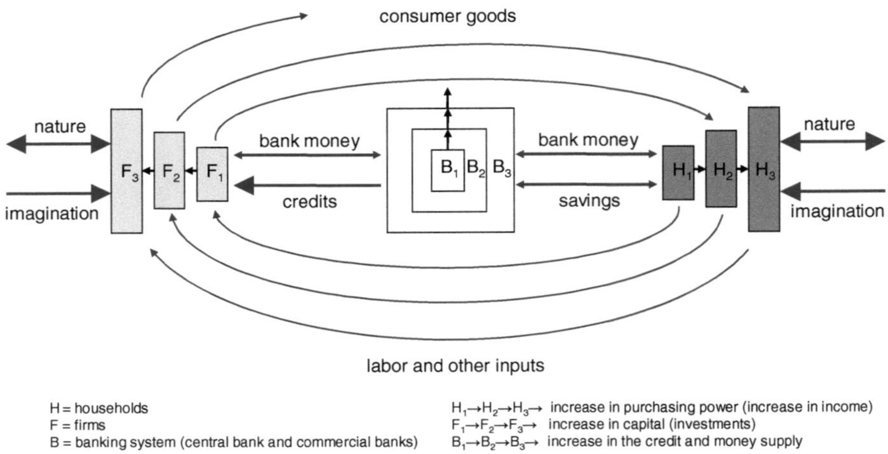

Fig. 9.1 The growth spiral

The growth spiral shows that the goal of the modern economy is not primarily achieving an optimal use of given resources but to expand the production from period to period by constantly increasing the use of natural resources with the help of human imagination and by money creation based on credits in the banking system.

This means that we cannot explain the production and distribution process without the time dimension. The neglect of time may be possible in a stationary economy where circular flows prevail. There, flows come always back to their initial state. But in a growing economy where the state of the economy at the end of a period is always different from the state at the beginning, the sequence of time must always be taken into account.

The recognition of the time dimension of the economic process allows us to explain the dynamism of a growing economy governed by a constant incentive for growth, which we have called growth impetus, as well by the necessity of growth, which we have called growth imperative. The growth process turns into a shrinking process if the growth process does not continue infinitely. This implies that zero growth is not feasible as soon as the growth process has been started. In the modern economy, we have only two alternatives: growing or shrinking (cf. Fig. 9.2).

This is different in a Robinson Crusoe economy, that is, in a self-sufficient or barter economy. Robinson can dispose at will of the use of his time and of the land he possesses. He can be content with maintaining the amount of consumption available from today's production or he can increase the consumption possibilities in the future by investing part of his time for the improvement of cultivation methods. In order to decide on the optimal use of his time, he will compare the additional utility coming from increased consumption possibilities in the future

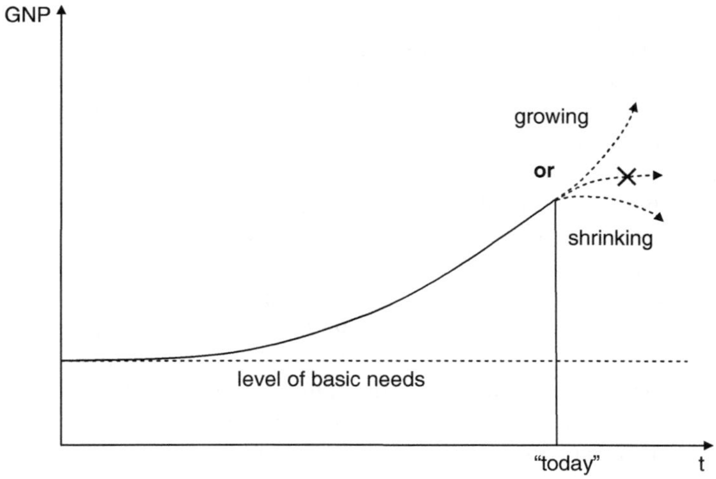

Fig. 9.2 The two alternatives: growing or shrinking

with the foregone consumption today, resulting from spending a smaller amount of his time for today's production. The result will depend only on his individual preferences. Whether expand production or not depends on Robinson Crusoe's own decisions. This freedom of decision is one of the advantages of self-sufficiency. It results from the fact that the self-sufficient household can dispose at will of his own products and of his own work effort.[1]

This freedom is no longer given if the traditional economy with self-sufficient households is replaced by a monetary economy. The restriction on the freedom of decision is, in a certain sense, the flip side of the expansion that results from the introduction of money as a means of payment, the possibility of capitalizing the money, and the continuous creation of new markets. This has led to a tremendous expansion of the amount of products and production but also to the imperative of further growth.

[1] The Robinson Crusoe-like method of economic management in earlier centuries is also the reason why, at a time when the majority of the population in Europe were self-sufficient farmers, there was no growth imperative. As a result, individual periods of growth, which arose through the influx of gold and silver and were facilitated by the use of energy—in particular the use of wind power for sailing and of hydropower for operating mills—could alternate with long periods of stagnation. It is therefore, as Rolf Peter Sieferle states, a mistake to assume that in earlier centuries there had already been continuous growth at a constant rate. Sieferle underlines this finding with a backward calculation of the social product on the basis of a constant rate of growth, with the result that: "If one extrapolates in reverse . . . the rate of natural growth of the age of industrialisation, as calculated by economic historians, one arrives, over longer periods of time, at a starting level well below any hope of subsistence. Therefore, historically speaking, something must have changed" (Sieferle 2003, p. 21). The historical change that he mentions is, of course, the monetarization and capitalization of the economy.

To recapitulate, the growth process is based on the time dimension of the market process, that is, on the necessity of prefinancing production with the help of an advance, named capital. In the market firms interact with private households. The firms are artificial economic units whose existence begins with the transformation of money into capital. The money that is to become capital must be provided by the capital owners. This is true not only for the borrowed capital but also for the equity capital. The borrowed capital is lent essentially from banks in the form of credits, whilst the equity capital is obtained from the households by issuing shares. The difference is that the borrowed capital is repayable whereas the equity capital is nonrepayable. The risk of banks is that their credits might not be repaid. The risk of the shareholders is that the shares may suffer losses of value in the stock market. In return for these risks, a *quid pro quo* must be provided. This *quid pro quo* is in both cases a stake in the firms' profits. For the banks this takes the form of interest paid on credits. For the shareholder it is the net profit which is in part paid out as a dividend and in part reinvested and, by way of this reinvestment, leads to an expected increase in the value of prices of the shares. Therefore, a surplus of money in the form of profits must always be achieved. This encompasses both the interest for borrowed capital and the net profit for equity capital.

The prerequisites for the existence of a firm as an artificial economic unit are therefore completely different from those for the existence of a private household or a natural person. In order for the latter to continue to exist, it is enough that his or her income covers subsistence costs. A surplus in excess of that minimum is welcome but not a condition for his or her very existence. On the other hand, the achievement of company profits, that is, a "more" in the form of earnings exceeding expenditures, is the indispensable prerequisite for the existence of a firm, irrespective of how high the absolute levels of the returns on capital are. The only thing that matters is this "more," more in excess of the capital invested.

The conclusion to be drawn from this is firms can only be founded when expectations for firm profits are positive, that is, the prospects of gain are higher than the risks of loss. Positive expectations result from past experience which has shown that, on average, gains have always been greater than losses.

As both earnings and expenditures of firms, and thus also their difference in the form of profits, are the result of monetary transactions, it follows that positive profits accrue if more money is earned than spent. This can only be if there is a constant influx of money. Thanks to the "Trick of Reason" (Hegel), the market process is arranged in such a way that the accrual of profits, which is essential in order to compensate the risk of capital investment, is made possible by the expansion of the investments financed on the basis of money creation. In turn, investments are motivated by the accrual of profits resulting from money creation.

This is explained by the spiral nature of the growing economy, that is, by the fact that investments instantly lead to an increase in the incomes of the households, whereas the higher production volumes, achieved as a result of the investments, only come onto the market tomorrow, that is, at a later date. The households therefore buy today what was produced yesterday. In this way the increase in demand always precedes the increase in supply. Accordingly, the earnings of firms that result from the demand of the households are always higher than the expenditures incurred for the products that the firms offer on the market.[2] The difference between the aggregate earnings and the aggregate expenditures is the aggregate profits of firms.

These aggregate profits may be distributed very unequally among the individual firms, however. This distribution greatly depends on the skill of the entrepreneur or on the market situation in which the individual firms finds itself. Some firms may also suffer losses. The essential thing is that, in the spiral of the growth process, firms' profits are made in the aggregate due to the continuous investment process that is promoted by expanding credit and money creation.

We thus arrive at the conclusion that, in the aggregate, the modern economy is founded on both, a growth impetus and a growth imperative. There is an impetus for growth, because an ongoing investment process does not only lead to an increase in current profits but also to an increase in the present value of shares in relation to the expected future profits. There is a growth imperative because, without a continuation of the investment process, that is an increase in capital investments, firms' profits would shrink continuously so that investors would no longer find it worthwhile to bear the risks associated with their investments. In the end, they would no longer be willing to finance replacement investments so that the stock of capital and therefore also both production and the incomes of the households would decrease. This process is accelerated as soon as interest payments can no longer be paid, because the firm is then threatened with bankruptcy. These findings result in the necessity of a positive rate of growth that must be sufficiently high to ensure that there are positive net profits which the owners of equity capital demand as a compensation for the risk that they are taking and also to ensure that interest payments can always be honored. This means that the increase in net profits and interest payments must, at a minimum, correspond to the increase in capital and that, vice versa, the increase in the volume of money that is triggered by the increase

[2] This assessment relates, in a certain sense, to the differentiation between the income and the production (capacity) effect of investments that is fundamental to the post-Keynesian theory of growth. The latter is also characterized by the time lag between the two effects. The post-Keynesian theory, however, considers only the real economy, whereas for us it is the monetary side of the economy that is decisive. Nevertheless, also E. D. Domar points out that a constant influx of money is essential to the growth process: "It is not sufficient . . . that savings of yesterday be invested today, or, as it is often expressed, that investments offset savings. Investment today must always exceed the saving of yesterday . . . An injection of new money . . . must take place every day" (Domar 1957, p. 92).

in capital must be high enough in order to make possible the corresponding increases in net profit and interest payments, which together make up the firms' profits.[3]

[3] A similar description of these facts can be found in Ernst Dorfner: "Let us, for the sake of simplicity, work . . . with a model assuming that all the money that the entrepreneurs invest in their production is money borrowed from money lenders. If the latter lend 100, then, at a rate of 10 % interest, they will expect to receive 110 after a year. The incorporation of the rate at which money circulates does not make any difference. All the money that the entrepreneurs require and which is present in the economy is . . . pre-financed by loans . . . Then only the amount of borrowed money can be repaid and not a single mark more. A hundred mark bill remains simply a hundred mark bill, no matter how many hands it passes through, no matter how quickly it circulates. And once it has been repaid, the hundred mark bill only returns to circulation if a new loan is taken out. It may indeed be possible that, with the aid of a new loan, the former interest may at first be repaid, but, as a result of this, a new debt is incurred together with a new demand for interest. In other words: interest payments demand an increase in the existing amount of money. Interest cannot simply come about as a result of redistribution or increase in the rate at which an existing amount of money circulates. . . . It may be distributed differently, but it has remained the same in total." Without an increase in the amount of money "a market economy is simply not able to function at all. . . . It would not only not be possible for any interest payment to be received and paid, but profits, too, could only be paid up to the amount of losses. .. The unsuccessful entrepreneurs would drop out of the economic process. A merciless process of selection with all its economic and social consequences would then take place at an ever increasing pace and quickly lead to the collapse of the entire system. . . . We can therefore take it for granted that interest payments and the average profits must represent a surplus, i.e. something gained in addition to that what already existed, and therefore cannot be the result of a process of redistribution. In the terms of game theory, this means, that our economy is not a zero-sum game like a card game in which the gains of one player are the losses of another. In the market economy game, the players return in the aggregate with profits, some with higher profits, some with lower profits, and a few may also suffer losses" (Dorfner 1994, 136ff.).

10 The Increase of the Present Value of Profits as the Growth Impetus

An essential component of the modern monetary system is the existence of a credit market with a relatively stable market rate of interest. This is based on the interest rate for public loans that, for simplicity, are considered to be risk-free, as the state can, if needed, always borrow money from its own central bank and therefore cannot go bankrupt in terms of its own money. It is therefore presumed that an owner of money will capitalize the money that he does not immediately need for consumption. By capitalizing we mean that he will invest it expecting to receive a return at a market rate at least equivalent to the interest rate for public loans.

The capital value is equivalent to the present value B_0 of the expected returns on the money invested K_0, plus the present value of the invested money to be repaid at the end of time period for which the money has been invested.

The capital value of the money that is not used in the same period in which it is earned is therefore

- less than the cash value of the money if it is horded (the difference between the cash value and the capital value is equal to the opportunity costs of holding or hording money)
- equal to the cash value of the money if it is invested at the market rate of interest r
- higher than the cash value if it is invested with an expected return e that exceeds the market rate of interest.

This would mean that for an investment over a period of 1 year, the present value B_0^1 (= capital value) of the invested money K_0 is

if $e = 0$

$$B_0^1 = \frac{0}{1+r}K_0 + \frac{K_0}{1+r} = \frac{K_0}{1+r} < K_0,$$

H.C. Binswanger, *The Growth Spiral*, DOI 10.1007/978-3-642-31881-8_10,

if $e = r$

$$B_0^1 = \frac{r}{1+r}K_0 + \frac{K_0}{1+r} = \frac{1+r}{1+r}K_0 = K_0,$$

and if $e > r$

$$B_0^1 = \frac{e}{1+r}K_0 + \frac{K_0}{1+r} = \frac{1+e}{1+r}K_0 > K_0.$$

Therefore, the following applies: When viewed as capital, money is only what it is if it becomes *more* than it *is*. And vice versa: If it does not become *more* than it *is*, then it will no longer be what it *is!* In the case of paper or bank money without an intrinsic value, failure to invest leads to a loss in value.

This statement does not apply to gold and silver money as the nominal value of gold and silver money is equivalent to its precious metal content. The value of gold and silver does not diminish if they are not invested as they have an intrinsic value which does not depend on the expected return from investing them.

If the profit rate is higher than the rate of interest, the present value of the capital invested increases with the time horizon of the investment. This may be explained as follows:

First: The present value of capital invested for an infinite period of time is greater than the present value of the capital invested that has to be repaid at the end of a finite period of time. This becomes evident when we compare these two present values.

The present value B_0^n of a capital invested for a limited period of n years is calculated according to the following formula, whereby j stands for the profit rate on equity capital invested:

$$\begin{aligned} B_0^n &= \frac{(1+r)^n - 1}{r(1+r)^n} jK_0^E + \frac{1}{(1+r)^n}K_0^E \\ &= \left[\frac{j}{r} - \frac{1}{(1+r)^n}\left(\frac{j}{r} - 1\right)\right]K_0^E. \end{aligned}$$

The present value B_0 of a sum invested for an infinite period of time ($n \to \infty$) is

$$B_0^\infty = \frac{j}{r}K_0^E.$$

If we assume that the profit rate is greater than the interest rate, that is

$$\frac{j}{r} > 1$$

we get

$$\frac{j}{r} - \frac{1}{(1+r)^n}\left(\frac{j}{r} - 1\right) < \frac{j}{r},$$

and therefore,

$$B_0^n < B_0^\infty.$$

This can be illustrated with an example. We set the values as follows:

$$r = 0.05,$$
$$j = 0.1,$$

$$K_0^E = 100.$$

If $n = 1$, the present value is

$$B_0^1 = \frac{1.10}{1.05} 100 \approx 105.$$

If $n \to \infty$, however, the present value is

$$B_0^\infty = \frac{0.10}{0.05} 100$$
$$= 200.$$

Therefore, there is a permanent incentive not to demand repayment of the invested equity capital but to perpetuate the investment. In this way, the growth process resulting from the investments may continue infinitely.

Second: The present value of the profits coming from investment in equity capital can be increased further, if a part c of the profit is not paid out as a dividend but reinvested.

If a part of the profits jK_t^E, amounting to cjK_t^E, is retained, the dividend does indeed decrease to $(1 - c)jK_t^E$. However, the equity capital increases by that part of the profits that is reinvested, namely, by cjK_t^E so that

$$K_t^E = (1 + cj)^t K_0^E.$$

When the equity capital increases, then this increase is equivalent to the increase in the expectations regarding dividends in the future. The present value of the increased capital B_0^w is thus equivalent to that of a perpetually increasing dividend. This is equivalent to the dividend share $(1 - c)$ of the profits jK_0^E. The present value of a perpetually increasing dividend B_0^w is calculated as the sum of the perpetually increasing dividends discounted to today[1]. Assuming all parameters remain constant, this will, at a given point in time 0, be

$$B_0^w = \frac{1}{r - cj}(1 - c)jK_0^E.$$

In contrast, the sum of a perpetually constant dividend B_0^∞ is, if the capital invested remains the same:

$$B_0^\infty = \frac{1}{r}jK_0^E.$$

If we now compare B_0^w with B_0^∞, we find that, even though

$$jK_0 > (1 - c)jK_0,$$

we nevertheless always have

$$B_0^\infty < B_0^w,$$

because

$$\frac{j}{r} < \frac{(1 - c)j}{r - cj}$$

or, after rearranging,

$$1 < \frac{r - cr}{r - cj}.$$

This is if, as assumed, $j > r$.

If we return to our example before and assume additionally that 30 % of the profits are reinvested ($c = 0.3$), then the present value B_0^w of the dividends is three and a half times the original capital investment, namely,

$$B_0^w = \frac{1}{0.02}0.07 \times 100$$
$$= 350.$$

[1] The present value, that is, the sum of the geometric progression of an infinitely increasing rent, is only finite if $r > cj$. This problem is known in the literature. M. H. Miller and F. Modigliani write on this subject: "The essential thing is, of course, that the present value is finite, which may always be assumed in an economic analysis" (Miller and Modigliani 1975, p. 293).

As opposed to this, the present value B_0^{∞} of a dividend equivalent to the undiminished profits is, provided all other conditions remain the same, only twice as high as the capital invested, namely, as has already been calculated,

$$B_0^{\infty} = 200.$$

The prospect of a constant reinvestment of a part of the profits therefore has the effect that the present value of the dividend from a perpetual investment that is already twice as high as the sum of the money invested increases by a further 75 %.

Inasmuch as it is possible to sell the capital investment on the capital market at its present value—this applies particularly to assets such as shares in public companies—this capital value can be realized at any time through selling the assets on the capital market. The foregoing of a part of the dividends is thus always overcompensated by the increase in the price of the assets resulting from the increase in the present values.

When reinvestments are made, the present value increases in accordance with the increase in equity capital thanks to the constant reinvestments from $B_{0,0}^{w}$ at time 0 to $B_{t,0}^{w}$ at time t

($t = 1, 2, \ldots$), that is, from

$$B_{0,0}^{w} = \frac{1-c}{r-cj} jK_0^E$$

to

$$\begin{aligned} B_{t,0}^{w} &= \frac{1-c}{r-cj} jK_t^E \\ &= \frac{1-c}{r-cj} (1+cj)^t jK_0^E. \end{aligned}$$

In our example, the capital $K_t^E = (1+cj)^t K_0^E$ increases

From today	100
to:	
After 10 years	134
After 20 years	180
After 30 years	242
After 40 years	326
After 50 years	438
↓	↓
The present value $B_{t,0}^w$ increases accordingly with the increasing capital	
From today	350
From today	350
to:	
After 10 years	470
After 20 years	632
After 30 years	850
After 40 years	1,142
After 50 years	1,534
↓	↓

The continued foregoing of a part of the profits leads, over the course of time, to a constantly increasing rate of growth of the capital value. The resulting impetus to grow therefore becomes stronger and stronger as time goes by.

By financing investments by bank loans, it is possible to further increase the return on equity capital. One speaks, in this context, of the leverage effect. Its magnitude depends upon the ratio between equity and borrowed capital. If we assume that the original profit rate on equity capital is j' where $j' > r$, then, by introducing borrowed capital, the profit rate on equity capital, and with it the net profit, increases, even if the profit rate for the total capital $K_0 (= K_0^E + K_0^F)$ remains constant at j'. The new profit rate on equity capital, j, is then

$$j = j' + (j' - r)\frac{K_0^F}{K_0^E} > j'.$$

However, there are limits to the possibilities of leverages because the higher the leverage rate, the higher the risk of bankruptcy.[2]

[2] There have been many arguments over the relevance or irrelevance of the capital structure, that is, the ratio between external and equity capital, otherwise known as the debt–equity ratio in the literature on financing investments. The proposition of the irrelevance of the debt–equity ratio was put forward by Modigliani and Miller (1955). According to these authors, the irrelevance of the debt–equity ratio only affects the assessment of a firm when the sum of the equity and borrowed capital remains constant. The irrelevance theory is not valid if, as we assume, it is possible to enlarge the amount of the capital as a whole. In this case, the present value of the future profits does increase with an increase in debt financing. Cf. on this subject: Klaus Spremann (1991, 281 ff.).

The increase in the rate of profit on equity capital as a result of the leverage effect can be illustrated with the aid of an example. Let us assume that $r = 0.05$ and the equity capital originally invested $K_0^E = 100$. If we set $j' = 0.075$ and assume that the originally invested equity capital is complemented by borrowed capital of the same amount, so that $K_0^E = K_0^F = 100$, the result is

$$\begin{aligned} j &= 0.075 + (0.075 - 0.05)\frac{100}{100} \\ &= 0.1. \end{aligned}$$

We have already anticipated this result in our examples designed to explain the capitalization of profits; in other words, we have already presumed that borrowed capital has been deployed alongside equity capital.

The increase in the rate of profit on equity capital as a result of the possibility of adding money borrowed from banks has the consequence that investments in equity capital become even more attractive, so that an increasing amount of equity capital is indeed invested. This, in turn, leads again to an increased demand for borrowed capital.

We conclude that the attractiveness of investing in equity capital increases constantly along with the possibility of borrowing money. This leads to a constant impetus for growth. This impetus itself increases in the course of time to the same degree as the growth of the economy progresses.

11 The Avoidance of Losses as the Growth Imperative

Coauthor: Guido Beltrani

Due to the growth impetus induced by the expectations of growing profits and incomes, economic growth is not perceived as an imperative but has become a normal phenomenon. For this reason, we have to explain this growth imperative in detail.

As we already showed, the growth imperative means that there is a minimum growth rate that the economy should not undercut. Otherwise, growth will turn into a shrinking process. Should the growth rate fall short of that mark, the economy will slip into a self-perpetuating crisis with losses that lead to a continuous reduction of the social product.

Let us summarize again the reasons for the growth imperative. It originates from the necessity to produce the goods before they can be sold on the market. For this purpose the firms need an advance, that is, capital, in order to purchase labor, raw materials, energy, etc., that they need for their production. Whether this capital investment is profitable or will at least cover the costs will not be known before the products come to the market. This gives rise to a risk. In order to compensate this risk, the investors require a return in the form of profit or interest. This is, on the aggregate, only guaranteed if there is economic growth. In the following, we shall derive the minimum growth rate on the basis of a model.

A growth model must explain the economic process in subsequent periods. This means that all variables have to be "dated," that is provided with a time index t, by means of which their temporal sequence is identified. However, this is not sufficient. We also need to allow for the fact that, within a particular period of time and during the transition from one period to another, events may occur that alter the situation and thus the production and market processes in the next period. These processes will exert an influence on the situation of the subsequent period, and so on. If the relative changes from period to period remain constant, we call the resulting growth process stable or balanced. Otherwise, there is unstable or unbalanced growth.

We will be denoting both the activities that occur at the transition from period $t-1$ to period t as well as the activities within the period t with the suffix t.

H.C. Binswanger, *The Growth Spiral*, DOI 10.1007/978-3-642-31881-8_11,

At the center of a growth process are the investments. Our model must therefore contain all variables and their changes that are decisive for investments being made in order to increase production and national income.

Our model is based on the following assumptions:

- We are looking at a closed economy, that is, presuming that the world is a uniform currency area.
- The economy consists merely of three agents, namely, the firms, the banks, and the households. The state and its central bank are only active "in the background," in creating the conditions upon which growth is founded: the framework conditions for the market and the possibility of creating money. We also assume stable interest rates in the long term.
- Firms and banks are publicly held stock companies.
- All production takes place in firms. These require capital, that is, money as an advance, in order to be able to purchase production services—labor and resources (land, raw materials, and energy)—from the households. All of the households' production services are paid from these advances. The speed of the circulation of money (V) from the firms back to the firms again is one period ($V = 1$).
- Capital consists of equity and borrowed capital. Equity capital is provided by the households as shareholders, borrowed capital by the banks.
- The banks grant the firms loans, which the firms book as borrowed capital, and receive interest payments from the firms in return. This is the only source of income for the banks. They require production services from the households. We shall be referring to the labor provided to the banks as "service performances" in order to distinguish them from the "production services" required by the firms as the producers of goods. The only expenses incurred by the banks result from the payments for the service performances and the dividend payments made to the households. The service performances are—so we assume—proportionate to the loans and thus to the income from interest received by the banks. In order not to allow the model to become too complicated, specific conditions for the capital needs of the banks are not considered. It is merely presumed that the banks require both equity and borrowed capital. The equity capital is provided by the households—the shareholders—who receive dividends in return. The borrowed capital of the banks consists of the sight deposits that the firms and the households maintain with the banks. The banks do not need to pay any interest for the deposits, as these represent money.
- The households supply production services to the firms and service performances to the banks. The households are shareholders in both the firms and the banks. Their income consists of the remuneration for the production services that they provide to the firms and the service performances they supply to the banks, plus the dividend payments of the firms and the banks.
- We make a radical simplification by assuming that the firms will not be requiring any permanent industrial goods such as machinery and buildings. Accordingly, only circulating capital is being used that is "written off" at a rate of 100 % every

period. In this case, the costs of the production and the expenses of the firms are identical in every period.

- All money is bank money, that is, it consists of sight deposits held with the banks. From this it follows:
  - The granting of loans by the banks to the firms takes the form of an increase in the sight deposits which the firms hold with the banks.
  - The interest payments made by the firms to the banks lead to a reduction of the sight deposits of the firms.
  - The payments of the banks for the service performances provided by the households and the dividend payments made by the banks take the form of an increase in the sight deposits of the households.
  - The payments between the firms and the households are effected by a transfer of the corresponding sight deposits.
  - Repaid credits are always replaced by new ones.
- We assume that the firms or rather their shareholders save money only by reinvesting retained profits in the firm, whilst the dividends and all other forms of household income are used for consumption purposes. This means that all loans are bank loans. Households and firms maintain only sight deposits (= money) and no savings deposits at the banks. All loans are therefore based—and this is an important simplification—on the creation of credit that leads to the creation of money, that is, to a corresponding increase in the sight deposits and thus in the money supply.
- The equity capital of the banks must to a certain extent keep pace with the increase in debt, that is, with the sight deposits in our model. This leads to a transfer of funds from sight deposits, which represent money, to the equity capital which does not represent money. Therefore—as explained in Part I (cf. p. 43)—a portion of money is constantly removed from circulation.[1]

[1] A corresponding argument is to be found in Richard Douthwaite: "Under the current money creation system the amount of money in circulation has to rise, year after year, by a sum at least equivalent to the amount being removed from circulation by the bank as a result of interest payments. The amount removed is equal to the profits left to the banks after they have paid dividends to their shareholders . . ., invested in new equipments and met all their wages, salaries and other operating costs . . . These profits will be held in accounts in the banks' own name and unless they are put back into circulation by being spent or lent, the amount of money in circulation will fall. As a result, the business sector will show a loss and cut back its investment and borrowing, thus pushing the whole economic system into decline." This results in the conclusion: "The fact that the amount of money in circulation usually has to increase each year to enable interest to be paid means that the total value of sales in the economy has to go up to if the ratio of the money supply (and thus debt) to the volume of trading is to stay constant . . .. This analysis means that, due to the way money is put into circulation, we have an economic system that needs to grow or inflate constantly. This is a major cause of our system's continuous and insatiable need for economic growth. If ever growth fails to materialize, and inflation does not occur, the money supply will contract and the economy will move into recession" (Douthwaite 1999, 24 f.).

- We further assume that the reduction of the amount of money in circulation as a result of hording and the increase in money resulting from consumptive loans to the state and the households are balanced.
- A crucial assumption is the distinction of the production and the market period. We thereby make the following simplifications:
  - The firms undertake all transactions that lead to the conclusion of the accounting period and the compilation of the balance for that period at the beginning of the following period. This affects in particular the payment of interest to the banks, the booking of profits, and the payment of dividends.
  - The entire production that the firms produce within the period $t - 1$ is offered by them on the market in the period t, that is, the products are put on stock in period $t - 1$ and sold from stock in period t. The stocks are valued at their production costs, that is, the expenses incurred by the firms when purchasing the production services in the period $t - 1$. The production costs of the goods sold in the period t are thus equal to the expenses incurred by the firms in the period $t - 1$.
  - The entire income that the households receive in the period t is spent by them in that same period t in order to purchase the products being offered on the market in that period (and which were produced in the previous period).
  - For the sake of simplification, it is assumed that the warehouses are emptied at the beginning of a period so that they need not be included in the firms' balance sheet that is drawn up at the beginning of that period. In this case, the entire capital of the firms that is available at the beginning of a period consists of cash that is used to pay for the production services required in that period.
  - We assume that the tendency to price increases will be counterbalanced by rationalization and thus by a reduction in the unit costs, so that the price level remains stable. In this case, nominal growth is equivalent to real growth.

  Our model is based on the following variables:

K_t, the total amount of capital that the firms invest in order to purchase the production services

K_t^{E}, the equity capital of the firms or their shareholders (=households)

K_t^{B}, the borrowed capital of the firms (=loans from the banks)
whereby

$$K_t = K_t^{\mathrm{E}} + K_t^{\mathrm{B}} \tag{11.1}$$

I_t, the total investments of the firms (=increase in total capital)

I_t^{E}, the investments of the firms financed by equity capital (=increase in equity capital)

I_t^{B}, the investments of the firms financed by borrowed capital (=increase in borrowed capital)
whereby

$$I_t = I_t^{\mathrm{E}} + I_t^{\mathrm{B}} \tag{11.2}$$

and

$$I_t^{\mathrm{E}} = K_t^{\mathrm{E}} - K_{t-1}^{\mathrm{E}} \tag{11.3}$$

or

$$I_t^{\mathrm{B}} = K_t^{\mathrm{B}} - K_{t-1}^{\mathrm{B}} \tag{11.4}$$

G_t^{F}, the gain made by the firm (=firms' profit)

G_t, the gain assigned to the equity capital (=net profit)

R_t, the interest paid on the borrowed capital
whereby

$$G_t = G_t^{\mathrm{F}} - R_t \tag{11.5}$$

D_t, the dividend, that is, the part of the net profit paid to the owners of the shares (=households)
whereby

$$D_t = G_t - I_t^{\mathrm{E}} \tag{11.6}$$

P_t^{F}, the production costs that need to be prefinanced, that is, the income of the households from the sale of the production services
whereby

$$P_t^{\mathrm{F}} = K_t \tag{11.7}$$

P_t^{BA}, the costs for bank transactions, that is, the income of the households from the sale of the service performances incl. the dividends paid by the banks

Y_t, the income of the households from the sale of the production services to the firms, the sale of the service performances to the banks, and the dividends paid by the firms and the banks

so that

$$Y_t = P_t^{\mathrm{F}} + P_t^{\mathrm{BA}} + D_t \tag{11.8}$$

E_t, the revenues received by the firms from the sale of their products to the households (=firms' earnings)

whereby

$$E_t = Y_t \tag{11.9}$$

O_t, the expenses ("outgoings") of firms when purchasing the production services

whereby

$$O_t = P_t^{\mathrm{F}} \tag{11.10}$$

C_t, the prefinanced costs of the production of the firms

whereby

$$C_t = O_{t-1}. \tag{11.11}$$

The firms' profit that has been generated at the transition from the period $t - 1$ to the period t and is therefore given the suffix t (cf. p. 130 above) is

$$G_t^{\mathrm{F}} = E_{t-1} - C_{t-1}. \tag{11.12}$$

The firms are creditworthy only if they have enough equity capital at their disposal. From the banks' point of view, the equity capital represents the security for granting a loan. For the sake of simplicity, it is being assumed that the ratio between borrowed and equity capital in the firm is fixed:

$$K_t^{\mathrm{B}} = dK_t^{\mathrm{E}}, \tag{11.13}$$

whereby the debt coefficient d, that is, the ratio between borrowed and equity capital, is determined by the business practice of the banks regarding their risk policy.

The relationship between the interest and the borrowed capital invested in the previous period is as follows:

$$R_t = rK^{\mathrm{B}}_{t-1}, \tag{11.14}$$

and therefore,

$$r = \frac{R_t}{K^{\mathrm{B}}_{t-1}}.$$

The interest rate r is determined by the central bank taking into account a sufficient profit margin for the banks with a view to a—as far as possible inflation-free—continued growth of the economy.

Finally, it is being assumed that the banks will spend a fixed proportion of their revenues for the service performances of the households and the dividends:

$$P^{\mathrm{BA}}_t = bR_t, \tag{11.15}$$

and therefore,

$$b = \frac{P^{\mathrm{BA}}_t}{R_t}$$

and

$$1 - b = \frac{R_t - P^{\mathrm{BA}}_t}{R_t},$$

whereby b stands for the ratio between the expenses of the banks and the interests (=revenue) they receive from the firms. Accordingly, $1 - b$ is that part of the income from interests (=revenue) that is used to increase the equity capital of the banks and thus the rate at which money disappears from circulation.

In order to prepare the solution for the system of equations (11.1)–(11.15), we will define another three variables that are constant if growth is balanced:

j, the profit rate, that is, the ratio between the net profit G_t and the equity capital of the firm invested in the previous period K^{E}_{t-1}, namely,

$$j = \frac{G_t}{K^{\mathrm{E}}_{t-1}} \tag{11.16}$$

c, the reinvestment rate, that is, that part of the net profit of the firm, that is not paid out as a dividend, namely,

$$c = \frac{I_t^{\mathrm{E}}}{G_t} = \frac{K_t^{\mathrm{E}} - K_{t-1}^{\mathrm{E}}}{G_t} \tag{11.17}$$

g^{E}, the growth rate of the equity capital, namely,

$$g^{\mathrm{E}} = \frac{I_t^{\mathrm{E}}}{K_{t-1}^{\mathrm{E}}} = \frac{K_t^{\mathrm{E}} - K_{t-1}^{\mathrm{E}}}{K_{t-1}^{\mathrm{E}}} \tag{11.18}$$

From the definition of these three variables, it follows that the growth rate of the equity capital is equivalent to the product of the reinvestment rate and the profit rate because

$$g^{\mathrm{E}} = \frac{I_t^{\mathrm{E}}}{G_t} \frac{G_t}{K_{t-1}^{\mathrm{E}}} = \frac{I_t^{\mathrm{E}}}{K_{t-1}^{\mathrm{E}}} = cj. \tag{11.19}$$

The reinvestment rate c is the strategic variable within the growth process. At a given rate of profit, it determines the rate of growth. If growth is balanced, all variables grow at the same constant rate. The growth rate of the equity capital g^{E} is then equal to the growth rate of the borrowed capital g^{B} and thus also equal to the growth rate of the total capital g^{K} and to the growth rate of the social product or national income g, namely,

$$g^{\mathrm{E}} = g^{\mathrm{B}} = g^{\mathrm{K}} = g = cj. \tag{11.20}$$

Equations (11.1)–(11.15) represent a linear system of 15 equations for the 16 variables $K_t, I_t, I_t^{\mathrm{E}}, I_t^{\mathrm{F}}, G_t, D_t, P_t^{\mathrm{F}}, Y_t, E_t, O_t, C_t, G_t^{\mathrm{F}}, K_t^{\mathrm{B}}, R_t, P_t^{\mathrm{BA}}$, and K_t^{E}.[2] It is known, however, that a system of equations that contains fewer equations than variables is underdefined. The system therefore describes a whole bundle of possible growth paths. In order to derive the minimum growth rate in a given context, the equations must be extended by a further condition. We derive this further condition as follows:

The modern economy is based upon the continuous generation and reinvestment of profits. Shareholders will only invest if they can expect to achieve a minimal profit covering the investment risk. If we define the corresponding minimum profit rate as $j_{\min}$, then the minimum profit must be

$$G_t = j_{\min} K_{t-1}^{\mathrm{E}}. \tag{11.21}$$

[2] It should be taken into account that many of the equations set up here are of a purely definitional nature. Only equations (11.3), (11.4), (11.11), (11.12), and (11.14) contain time lags and are therefore "true" difference equations.

The minimum reinvestment rate $c_{\min}$ and the minimum growth rate $g_{\min}$ are the result of resolving the equation system (11.1)–(11.15) and (11.21).

We shall begin with equation (11.12) $G_t^{\mathrm{F}} = E_{t-1} - C_{t-1}$ which determines the firms' profits as a residual value. This is calculated at the end of the period $t - 1$ from the difference between the revenue E_{t-1} of the firms that is the result of the sales of products in period $t - 1$ and the costs C_{t-1} of the products sold during period $t - 1$.

In order to determine the net profit, the interest payments must be subtracted from the firms profit in accordance with Eq. (11.5). According to Eq. (11.14), the interest payments are in relation to the borrowed capital: $R_t = rK_{t-1}^{\mathrm{B}}$. If these values are inserted into Eq. (11.5), the result is

$$G_t = E_{t-1} - C_{t-1} - rK_{t-1}^{\mathrm{B}}. \tag{11.22}$$

The revenue of the firms E_{t-1} is equal to the income of the households Y_{t-1} so that according to Eq. (11.9),

$$E_{t-1} = Y_{t-1}.$$

According to Eq. (11.8), the income of the households in the period $t - 1$ is made up of three components, namely:

- The income P_{t-1}^{F} that the households earn as remuneration for the production services they have provided in the period $t - 1$
- The income P_{t-1}^{BA} that is paid to them by the banks as a remuneration for the service performances they have provided and as dividends in the period $t - 1$
- The income D_{t-1} which they receive from the firms as dividends in the period $t - 1$

The revenues of the firms from the sale of the products in the period $t - 1$ are confronted by the costs C_{t-1} of the products in the same period $t - 1$. These were carried forward by the firms from the previous period $t - 2$ to the period $t - 1$ with the sum which they had paid for the production. This means that the products were put on stock in period $t - 2$ and sold from stock in period $t - 1$. The stocks are valued at their production costs. The costs of the products that are sold in the period $t - 1$ are therefore equivalent to the expenses ("outgoings") O_{t-2} or rather the production costs P_{t-2}^{F} of the period $t - 2$ [cf. Eqs. (11.10) and (11.11)].

If we then replace in Eq. (11.22) E_{t-1} with $P_{t-1}^{\mathrm{F}} + P_{t-1}^{\mathrm{BA}} + D_{t-1}$ and C_{t-1} with P_{t-2}^{F}, the result is

$$G_t = P_{t-1}^{\mathrm{F}} + P_{t-1}^{\mathrm{BA}} + D_{t-1} - P_{t-2}^{\mathrm{F}} - rK_{t-1}^{\mathrm{B}}. \tag{11.23}$$

The three income components P_{t-1}^{F} (and P_{t-2}^{F} respectively), P_{t-1}^{BA}, and D_{t-1} are determined as follows:

- The income of the households, P_{t-1}^{F}, which they receive from the firms for the *production services* they have performed during the period $t - 1$, is paid from the total capital K_{t-1} that was invested at the beginning of the period $t-1$ [Eq. (11.7)].

- The income of the households P^{BA}_{t-1}, which they receive from the banks for the *service performances plus dividends* provided by the banks, can be regarded as a fixed part of the interest revenues of the banks [Eq. (11.15)].
- The *dividend income* D_{t-1} that the households receive from the firms is the part of the net profit that is not reinvested [Eq. (11.6)].

It therefore follows from Eq. (11.23) that

$$G_t = K_{t-1} + bR_{t-1} + G_{t-1} - I^{\mathrm{E}}_{t-1} - K_{t-2} - rK^{\mathrm{B}}_{t-1}. \tag{11.24}$$

The interest R_{t-1} relates to the borrowed capital according to Eq. (11.14) as follows:

$$R_{t-1} = rK^{\mathrm{B}}_{t-2}.$$

I^{E}_{t-1} corresponds, according to Eq. (11.3), to the increase in equity capital between the periods $t-2$ and $t-1$:

$$I^{\mathrm{E}}_{t-1} = K^{\mathrm{E}}_{t-1} - K^{\mathrm{E}}_{t-2}.$$

It therefore follows from Eq. (11.24) that

$$G_t = K_{t-1} + brK^{\mathrm{B}}_{t-1} + G_{t-1} - (K^{\mathrm{E}}_{t-1} - K^{\mathrm{E}}_{t-2}) - K_{t-2} - rK^{\mathrm{B}}_{t-1}. \tag{11.25}$$

The total capital is made up of the equity capital K^{E}_t and borrowed capital K^{B}_t [Eq. (11.1)]. The borrowed capital K^{B}_t that is invested in the period t is itself proportional to the equity capital invested, that is, in accordance with Eq. (11.13), $K^{\mathrm{B}}_t = dK^{\mathrm{E}}_t$, and therefore,

$$K_t = (1+d)K^{\mathrm{E}}_t,$$

and therefore, finally,

$$\begin{aligned} G_t - G_{t-1} &= dK^{\mathrm{E}}_{t-1} + brdK^{\mathrm{E}}_{t-2} - dK^{\mathrm{E}}_{t-2} - rdK^{\mathrm{E}}_{t-1} \\ &= (1-r)dK^{\mathrm{E}}_{t-1} - (1-br)dK^{\mathrm{E}}_{t-2}. \end{aligned} \tag{11.26}$$

If we insert Eq. (11.21) in Eq. (11.26), then it follows that

$$j_{\min}K^{\mathrm{E}}_{t-1} - j_{\min}K^{\mathrm{E}}_{t-2} = (1-r)dK^{\mathrm{E}}_{t-1} - (1-br)dK^{\mathrm{E}}_{t-2}$$

or

$$[(1-r)d - j_{\min}]K^{E}_{t-1} = [(1-br)d - j_{\min}]K^{E}_{t-2} \tag{11.27}$$

or

$$K^{E}_{t-1} = \frac{[(1-br)d - j_{\min}]K^{E}_{t-2}}{(1-r)d - j_{\min}}. \tag{11.28}$$

This leads us to the balanced minimum growth rate $g^{E}_{\min}$ of the equity capital:

$$\begin{aligned} g^{E}_{\min} &= \frac{K^{E}_{t-1} - K^{E}_{t-2}}{K^{E}_{t-2}} \\ &= \frac{(1-b)rd}{d - j_{\min} - rd}. \end{aligned} \tag{11.29}$$

When growth is balanced, the growth rates of all variables must be the same so that the same result also applies to the balanced minimum growth rate of the total capital and thus the social product. Thus, we receive as the result of the solution of the system of equations

$$\boxed{g_{\min} = \frac{(1-b)rd}{d - j_{\min} - rd}.} \tag{11.30}$$

The minimum balanced rate of reinvestment is, according to Eq. (11.20),

$$c_{\min} = \frac{g_{\min}}{j_{\min}} = \frac{(1-b)rd}{(d - j_{\min} - rd)j_{\min}}. \tag{11.31}$$

Under the condition that

$$d(1-r) - j_{\min} > 0,$$

the minimum balanced growth rate $g_{\min}$ is greater than zero because:

- The banks must make a profit in order to stay in business so that

$$b < 1.$$

- The banks will only grant loans if they receive interests that are in a fixed proportion to the loan (borrowed capital) so that

$$r > 0.$$

The meaning of the equation for the minimum rate of growth becomes evident when we bear in mind that the borrowed capital is generated from the money-creating process within the banking system and that, therefore, the growth of borrowed capital is identical with the growth in the money supply that results from the lending process of the banks. This tells us that the creation of money within a period must be sufficiently high, such that:

- The necessary growth of minimum net profits is achieved.
- The increase in interests can be paid.
- And, at the same time, the money removed from circulation is replaced.

We arrive at this result when we multiply the formula for the minimum growth rate with the equity capital K^{E}_{t-1}. The extended equation reads as

$$g_{\min}K^{\mathrm{E}}_{t-1} = \frac{(1-b)rd}{d - j_{\min} - rd}K^{\mathrm{E}}_{t-1},$$

or, after rearranging,

$$\begin{aligned}(c_{\min}\, j_{\min})dK^{\mathrm{E}}_{t-1} = (c_{\min}\, j_{\min})\, j_{\min}K^{\mathrm{E}}_{t-1} + (c_{\min}\, j_{\min})rdK^{\mathrm{E}}_{t-1} \\ + (1-b)rdK^{\mathrm{E}}_{t-1},\end{aligned} \tag{11.32}$$

whereby

- $(c_{\min}\, j_{\min})dK^{\mathrm{E}}_{t-1}$ is the increase in borrowed capital at the beginning of period $t-1$ (money creation at the beginning of the period):

$$(c_{\min}\, j_{\min})dK^{\mathrm{E}}_{t-1} = \frac{K^{\mathrm{B}}_{t} - K^{\mathrm{B}}_{t-1}}{K^{B}_{t-1}}K^{\mathrm{F}}_{t-1} = K^{\mathrm{B}}_{t} - K^{\mathrm{B}}_{t-1}.$$

- $(c_{\min}\, j_{\min})j_{\min}K^{\mathrm{E}}_{t-1}$ is the required increase in minimum net profits at the end of the period:

$$(c_{\min}\, j_{\min})j_{\min}K^{\mathrm{E}}_{t-1} = \frac{G_{t+1} - G_{t}}{G_{t}}G_{t} = G_{t+1} - G_{t}.$$

- $(c_{\min}\, j_{\min})rdK^{\mathrm{E}}_{t-1}$ is the increase in interests at the end of the period:

$$c_{\min}\, j_{\min}rdK^{\mathrm{E}}_{t-1} = \frac{R_{t+1} - R_{t}}{R_{r}}R_{t} = R_{t+1} - R_{t}.$$

- $(1-b)rdK^{\mathrm{E}}_{t-1}$ is the money removed from circulation:

$$(1-b)rdK^{\mathrm{E}}_{t-1} = (1-b)R_{t}.$$

These findings also explain the inequality already presumed above:

$$d(1-r) - j_{\min} > 0, \tag{11.33}$$

which must apply in order for the growth rate to have a positive value. By multiplying $d(1-r) - j_{\min} > 0$ with K_{t-1}^{E}, we obtain the inequality

$$dK_{t-1}^{\mathrm{E}} > j_{\min} K_{t-1}^{\mathrm{E}} + rdK_{t-1}^{\mathrm{E}}.$$

This inequality states that the borrowed capital of firms dK_{t-1}^{E}, which is invested in the period $t-1$ and is equivalent to the money creation of banks up to the period $t-1$, must be higher than the profit at the beginning of the period t that remunerates the use of equity capital, plus the interest that is owed for the investment of borrowed capital during the period $t-1$.

We are now able to quantify how the minimum growth rate g_{min} depends upon the interest rate, the minimum profit rate, the debt coefficient, and the rate at which money is removed from circulation.

If we recall Eq. (11.30)

$$g_{\min} = \frac{(1-b)rd}{d - j_{\min} - rd},$$

we see that the minimum profit rate $g_{\min}$ is higher, the higher the interest rate r is. As there is a plus sign in the numerator and a minus sign in the denominator, the partial derivative is

$$\frac{\partial g_{\min}}{\partial r} > 0.$$

The necessary minimum profit rate has a minus sign in the numerator. The minimum growth rate is therefore higher, the higher the necessary minimum profit rate, that is,

$$\frac{\partial g_{\min}}{\partial j_{\min}} > 0.$$

In order to determine the dependency of the minimum growth rate upon the debt coefficient, we take the derivative of the growth formula with respect to d. The result of this is

$$\frac{\partial g_{\min}}{\partial d} = \frac{(1-b)r(d - j_{\min} - rd) - (1-b)rd(1-r)}{(d - j_{\min} - rd)} < 0.$$

The minimum growth rate $g_{\min}$ is therefore lower, the greater the debt coefficient. (Note, however, that the increase in the debt coefficient is limited by the increased risk that results from a higher amount of debt.)

The rate at which money is removed from circulation $(1-b)$ appears in the numerator with a plus sign. This means that the minimum growth rate is higher, the higher the rate at which money is removed, that is,

$$\frac{\partial g_{\min}}{\partial(1-b)} > 0.$$

As a result, the minimum growth rate has to be higher, the higher the interest rate, the higher the minimum profit rate and the higher the rate at which money is removed from circulation. On the other hand, the minimum growth rate is lower, the higher the debt coefficient, that is, the higher the ratio of external to equity capital, that is, the higher the inflow of money with each investment.[3]

We can illustrate the formula for the minimum balanced rate of growth by means of a plausible example that reflects the real situation in a fairly adequate manner. We will thereby be using the values for the interest rate r and the debt coefficient d that we have already used for the purpose of illustrating the growth impetus. Moreover, we will be assuming that the values used for the profit rate is the minimum profit rate. We therefore set

$$\begin{aligned} r &= 0.05 \\ d &= 1 \\ j_{\min} &= 0.1. \end{aligned}$$

In addition, it is necessary to calibrate the rate $(1-b)$ at which money is removed from circulation, as this plays a significant role in the formula for determining the minimum rate of growth. Taking into account the structure of the balance sheet of an "average" bank, we assume

$$1-b = 0.3.$$

The resulting minimum rate of growth amounts to

$$\begin{aligned} g_{\min} &= 0.018 \\ &= 1.8\,\%. \end{aligned}$$

As we consider the world as a single currency area, the growth rate in our example is to be regarded as a global rate of growth. Lower rates of growth in one

[3] At a given rate $(1-b)$ at which money is removed from circulation, a given minimum profit rate $(j_{\min})$, and a given debt coefficient (d), the minimum growth rate is mainly dependent upon the interest rate and is lower, the lower the interest rate is. But this does not necessarily mean that the actual growth rate is also lower. The reason is that the lower the rate of interest, the more advantageous it is for the firms to invest, and hence, the higher will be the effective growth rate. This means that when the interest rate goes down, the growth imperative is reduced, but the growth impetus increases.

country may be compensated by higher rates elsewhere. As it is possible now for capital to be invested everywhere, what matters is the worldwide (weighted) average growth rate of all countries.

This raises the question of what will happen if too little is invested and thus the rate of growth falls short of the minimum balanced rate of growth, be it because investments have become unattractive, be it because external reasons inhibit investments. The answer is sooner or later the firms will start making losses.

To explain this, we will assume that the reinvestment or investment rate, that is, the ratio between the investments financed with equity capital I_t^{E} and the net profit G_t, is already zero at the beginning of the period $t + 1$ so that

$$c_{t+1} = I_{t+1}^{\mathrm{E}}/G_{t+1} = 0.$$

In this case, the entire net profit will be consumed, whilst the equity capital in the period $t + 1$ remains the same as it had been in the period t. At a constant debt coefficient [cf. Eq. (11.13)], it follows that no new money is borrowed. Equity and borrowed capital remain the same as in period t so that $K_{t+1} = K_t$. It is also assumed that the rate of profit achieved corresponds to the minimum rate of profit, that is,

$$G_{t+1} = j_{\min}K_t^{\mathrm{E}}.$$

The income of the households in the period $t + 1$ is therefore

$$Y_{t+1} = (1 + d)K_t^{\mathrm{E}} + j_{\min}K_t^{\mathrm{E}} + brdK_t^{\mathrm{E}} \text{ [cf. Eq. (11.8)].}$$

In this case, the entire income is consumed, and so, the revenues of the firms E_{t+1} are equal to the incomes of the households, namely,

$$E_{t+1} = Y_{t+1}.$$

The firms sell the goods that they produced during period t and which are valued at the production costs P_t^{F} in the period t. These are equal to the capital invested during period t, that is,

$$\begin{aligned} P_t^{\mathrm{F}} &= K_t \\ &= (1 + d)K_t^{\mathrm{E}}. \end{aligned}$$

According to Eq. (11.12), the firms' profit G_{t+2}^{F} in period $t + 2$ that is determined by the sale of goods in the period $t + 1$ is thus

$$\begin{aligned} G_{t+2}^{\mathrm{F}} &= E_{t+1} - P_t^{\mathrm{F}} \\ &= (1 + d)K_t^{\mathrm{E}} + j_{\min}K_t^{\mathrm{E}} + brdK_t^{\mathrm{E}} - (1 + d)K_t^{\mathrm{E}} \\ &= (j_{\min} + brd)K_t^{\mathrm{E}}. \end{aligned}$$

This means that the net profit in the period $t + 2$ is

$$G_{t+2} = [j_{\min} - (1-b)rd]K_t^{\mathrm{E}}$$

and the profit rate j_{t+2}^{s} in the period $t + 2$, where j^{s} stands for the profit rate in case the reinvestment rate c is equal to zero, is

$$j_{t+2}^{s} = [j_{\min} - (1-b)rd] < j_{\min}.$$

The profit rate in the period $t + 2$ falls short of the minimum profit rate required.

Subsequently the profit rate continues to fall if no new investments are made and thus no new money is borrowed. This results from the fact that the interest rates for loans still have to be paid, which, in turn, leads to money disappearing from circulation at a rate of $(1-b)rdK_t^{\mathrm{E}}$ in each period. The amount of money disappearing from circulation accumulates over the course of time.

The earnings of the firms and therefore their profits are reduced by this amount. Accordingly, in the period $t + 3$ the profit rate is

$$j_{t+3}^{s} = j_{\min} - 2(1-b)rd,$$

and in the period $t + n$,

$$j_{t+n}^{s} = j_{\min} - (n-1)(1-b)rd.$$

If we return to our example, then the profit rate in the period $t + 2$ falls to

$$\begin{aligned} j_{t+2}^{s} &= 0.1 - 0.3 \times 0.05 \times 1 \\ &= 0.085. \end{aligned}$$

After eight periods, the profit is turned into an actual loss because

$$\begin{aligned} j_{t+8}^{s} &= 0.1 - 7(0.3 \times 0.05 \times 1) \\ &= 0.1 - 0.105 \\ &= -0.005. \end{aligned}$$

During these periods the share prices will continuously fall as a consequence of the falling profit rate, so that the assets of the shareholders already begin to shrink at a time when profits are still being made.

It should also be taken into account that the lower *average* rate of profit is composed of higher and lower rates of profit, and therefore, from period to period, losses are made by an ever-increasing number of firms. The losses, if they continue over a longer period of time, lead to bankruptcy and thus to a reduction in the money supply as the bankruptcy leads to the cancelation of the sight deposits of the enterprises. The shrinking process therefore starts already at a time when the *average* rate of profit is still positive.

Shorter phases with a profit rate that falls short of the minimum required profit rate may be absorbed by the economy. But, if the shrinking growth process continues for a longer period of time and there is no prospect of the economy starting to grow again, production will collapse and the economy threatens to shrink to Robinson Crusoe level.

12 Growth Opportunities and Growth Obstacles: The Role of the State

The growth impetus, characteristic of the modern economy, regularly causes the actual growth rate g to be higher than the minimum growth rate g_{min}:

$$g > g_{\text{min}}.$$

This is due to the fact that competition always induces firms to open up new growth opportunities. However, growth opportunities come along with growth obstacles. As we have previously argued in detail, these have been reduced in the last 200 years more and more. Nonetheless, these obstacles could not be entirely eliminated.

In the following, we want to recall the three most important growth obstacles that had dampened growth in the past and how the modern economy tried to get rid of them. We repeat what we have already explained before. But we will also discuss the shortcoming of these steps.

The three most important growth obstacles are:

- The scarcity of capital
- The limited supply of resources
- The saturation of people's wants

Acute *scarcity of capital*, resulting, in previous centuries, from the dependency of capital on savings, could be removed to a large extent through credit and money creation. The essential element of this creation is the conversion of debts into money. This occurs through banks granting credits in the form of sight deposits. Since sight deposits can be used for payment transactions, they are money. The sight deposits are debits of the banks, since they can be converted into banknotes (paper money). The latter are legal tender money, issued by the central bank. The banks can obtain banknotes in the form of credits from the central bank. Banknotes were to be considered as a debt of the central bank, because they were convertible into gold. But since the convertibility of banknotes into gold was suspended, the debt became a nonrepayable debt. As nonrepayable debt can be increased without limits, also money creation can be expanded without limits. As credits are mainly

H.C. Binswanger, *The Growth Spiral*, DOI 10.1007/978-3-642-31881-8_12,

given to firms and are used by firms for investment purposes, the scarcity of capital could to a great extent be surmounted.

The *finiteness of the supply of natural resources* was a limiting factor as long as land was the most important resource. The amount of this resource is (more or less) known and is divided among its owners. Only the owner (or someone who has rented it) can use the land and has the right to sell the fruit the land bears. Therefore, land has become a scarce resource not only physically but also economically. Nevertheless, its yield can be increased considerably by the use of energy-powered machines, chemicals, fertilizers, and the application of biotechnologies, implying that the scarcity of land does not manifest itself in a scarcity of yield.

The supply of raw material and energy, which are gained from mineral resources, is constantly increasing. The exploration of new supplies of raw material and energy gives rise to the allocation of new property rights and thus to a higher supply. The scarcity of raw materials and energy sources is therefore, from the perspective of the market, only of a temporary, not of a definitive, character. Thus, the supply of resources was growing for the last 200 years, even if the world and, with it, its physical stock of resources as a whole is limited. For this reason, prices could be kept on a relatively low level despite the permanent increase of demand.

Substituting labor by energy implies that full employment of labor is not a growth obstacle any more. As energy will remain relatively cheap compared to labor, the costs of production will not increase proportionally to wages. Hence, this has made it possible to eliminate wage increases as a growth obstacle.

There is still the open issue of the *saturation of* people's wants as a further possible growth obstacle. Such saturation is only conceivable for natural persons, for households, but not for firms as legal—artificial—entities. Whereas the increase in the number of natural persons in the world is slowing down, the number of firms as legal entities and their scope is increasing all the time. These "subsist" on investments. There is no saturation. On the contrary, the larger they become, the more "food," that is, investments, they need in order to stay alive. However, these investments are only profitable if the growing output, which is caused by investments, can be sold to the households, that is, to natural persons. Thus, the saturation point of the natural persons must be postponed constantly. Otherwise the economy will shrink. Therefore, it is an important management task of firms to choose successful marketing policies and to invent new products. "Consumer orientation" has become a major factor of success. It focuses on the human capability of imagination which, in principle, is unlimited.

Moreover, we can observe that, as Norbert Bolz (2002, p. 82) has put it, money itself incorporates the additional value of providing options to choose. Striving for money is therefore also induced by the very fact that the more money one possesses, the more opportunities for choosing there are. Striving for more and more money is therefore not limited by the current need for real goods.

The most extreme form of the elimination of the boundaries given by the saturation of wants is the demand for equity ownership, in particular in the form of shares which are valued according to future expectations. Since their present values increase with expected profits and thus with investments, which are intended to increase profits in the future, households are interested not only in present consumption but also in an increase in investments and thus in future profits. Thus, equity ownership becomes a "consumption good." That means the reinvestment of a portion of the firm's profits is not considered as saving, that is, as a forgoing of present consumption of goods, but as the *present* consumption of an *expected* value increase. The value increase is theoretically realizable at any point in time by selling the shares on the stock market. But, in fact, it is only realized reluctantly or not at all since this would imply forgoing further value increases.

The non-satiability of the rich for such imaginary goods is complemented by the non-satiation of the physical hunger of the poor. This non-satiation for real goods allows the increasing real production to be absorbed. But this can only occur if the poor are included in the growth spiral of the modern economy, that is, that the poor earn enough money to be able to purchase the increased production.

The overcoming of the saturation barrier therefore takes place on two levels. On the level of the rich and the potential saturated people; this occurs by the increase of imaginary goods as these remain mainly virtual. At the level of the poor, this happens by the gradual monetarization of incomes which allows the satiation of their hunger through purchases on the market. At the moment, overcoming the saturation barrier by the rich is of greater economic importance because the increase in present values of future profits proceeds faster than the inclusion of the poor into the growth spiral. An essential reason for the slowness of this process is the continuous substitution of labor by energy, so that the demand for labor increases at a slower pace than the increase in capital and the present values of future profits. Nevertheless, the rise of monetary incomes throughout the world remains an important precondition for economic growth.

However, certain growth obstacles could not be removed. This is due to several factors. These obstacles belong, on the one hand, to the monetary side of the economy and, on the other hand, to the real side of the economy, and in part also to both sides of the economy.

Growth obstacles can primarily occur in the *monetary sector*. This is due to the fact that money is divided into different currencies, with one particular currency functioning as the leading one. In the past, this was the English pound; today it is the US dollar. This division can give rise to disturbances. The country with the leading currency can go ahead with money and credit creation, since the other countries hold reserves in the leading currency. Furthermore, the latter is used as a means of payments beyond its own borders. Inflationary pressures, an excessive government debt, or a balance of payments deficit may nevertheless destroy the confidence in the leading currency. Consequently, the willingness to hold reserves in the leading currency and its use as a global means of payment will decrease. The resulting devaluation of the leading currency may force the central banks of the other countries to implement policies which are destabilizing their own economies.

Furthermore, degradation to second-class currencies may follow as a consequence of high inflation. These currencies would not be accepted for credits anymore. Then the governments can only issue debt which is denominated in the leading currency or in a currency which can be converted into the leading currency at a relatively stable exchange rate. If taxes are raised in the domestic currency, but its exchange rate is constantly falling due to inflation, while the interest rates are to be paid in the leading or in a convertible currency, this can lead to state bankruptcy.

International coordination efforts and international monetary organizations such as the International Monetary Fund (IMF) may mitigate but can also exacerbate these disturbing factors. The arbitrariness of decisions might result in inappropriate measures with respect to the given situation.

The imperfections of the monetary system can lead to an unpredictable destruction of capital. This might be due to inflation or deflation but also due to currency crises which are accompanied by a destabilization and a higher volatility of the exchange rates. The fundamental ability of the modern banking system to provide always sufficient capital can become uncertain under these circumstances.

In addition, growth obstacles may also result from disturbances in the *real sector,* if some natural resources get definitively scarce, if the replenishment of it does not occur in time since not enough capital has been provided for the exploration, or if the transition to substitutes causes high costs. This undermines the hierarchy of prices on which economic growth is based—low prices for energy and raw materials and high prices for the final products. The development of energy prices is of particular significance because the increased use of energy is the basis for most innovations. A rapid increase in energy prices disturbs the innovation activities. Current innovations may suddenly become obsolete. This will have a dampening effect on growth which is based on these innovations.

Further growth obstacles relate to both *the monetary and the real sector*. These include primarily the obstacles which result from the loss in value of the goods that are demanded by the rich. Within this range of products, the value of shares plays a central role. The demand for these can indeed grow without limits but only if a further increase in value is expected. However, this increase in value can suddenly turn into a loss if increases in demand for shares lead to price increases that exceed so-called fundamental values. Furthermore, for whatever reason, doubts may arise concerning the possibility to resell shares. In this case, the perspective of unlimited gains is replaced by the gaze into the abyss of losses. The demand for shares decreases and, with it, their values. At first, only accounting losses are made. However, under certain circumstances, these losses are transformed into real ones. This can be the case when the present value of shares has acted as a security for a loan. In this case, the decline in the present value can result in the cancelation of a credit or demand for additional payments that the borrower may not be able to comply with. A real loss is also incurred when the share owner is forced to sell because of an emergency whilst he bought the shares at a higher price. In the case of institutional investors who hold assets in present values in their balance sheets, the decline in present values leads to a reduction of profits or even to an actual loss. However, most importantly, if a firm loses its creditworthiness, investments cannot be made to the same extent as before, which, sooner or later, induces the firm to incur real losses.

In this context, the state is challenged. Its task is to support the growth orientation of the market. Consequently the state has made itself dependent on economic growth. The increasing expenditures which are related to economic growth can only be financed through increasing tax revenues stemming from increased profits and incomes or through gradually rising public debt. Revenues of profit and income taxes are only collected after they have been imposed, whereas the expenditures, which are drivers of economic growth, have to precede production. Thus, the augmentation of public debt becomes inevitable. However, if national debt increases, so does the interest burden which, in turn, can only be shouldered if revenues increase. Hence, the state has every reason to contribute for its own sake to the stimulation and the perpetuation of growth.

Nonetheless, the state is confronted with the negative external effects which are related to economic growth. These are, in particular:

- The increasing discrepancy between growth and employment which results from the substitution of labor by energy
- The unequal income distribution as a result of the different degrees of the inclusion of households in the growth process and the resulting social unrest
- The discrepancy between the levels of income of the industrialized nations and those of the developing countries whose access to the capital market is limited
- The environmental damages which stem from the accumulation of waste and emissions of all kinds, including a possible climate change and the disappearance of natural landscapes for recreation
- The herding together of an increasing number of people in so-called megacities due to a still continuous growth of the world population leading to a constant worsening of living conditions.

This development is necessarily followed by an increasing politicization of the economy, as the containment of the negative external effects may also lead to a limitation of growth. The state may, however, try to combine employment, social, environmental, and development policies with the support of economic growth. Growth allows for producing the financial means for these purposes. Other strategies are designed to make these policy areas more compatible with economic growth. This may, for example, result in an increase in the level of education in order to meet the demand for more high-skilled workers, in the improvement of the access of developing countries to capital markets, etc. But if these measures are insufficient, the state is in any case forced to give priority to growth.[1] The growth imperative also includes the state and does, under present conditions, not allow for any other alternative.

---

[1] Today, the justification of the modern state relates, to a large extent, to its ability to promote economic growth. cf. H. Tenne (1988, p. 43): "Since the rise of the modern state, economic growth has been central to the legitimacy of political authority. Continuous autonomous economic growth occurs with the evolution of the modern secular state and its political economies of growth." See also Reinhard Steuerer (2004, 378 ff).

Summary and Outlook 13

The modern economy is oriented towards growth. The quantity and number of products available for purchase is constantly increasing on a worldwide scale. Many of those who do not yet benefit from increased material wealth can hope to do so soon.

One important prerequisite for economic growth was the continuous replacement of barter by monetary exchanges, along with a simultaneous increase in the use of natural resources. In this way, the economic process was transformed into an open-ended upward-turning spiral.

The explanation of the dynamics of this growth spiral is the central theme of this book. In the following, we will first provide a summary of the main insights developed in this book. We will then conclude with an outlook on the opportunities as well as the risks entailed by the growth spiral.

For the understanding of the functioning of the modern economy, it is important to distinguish between barter economies and money-based market economies. In a certain sense, a barter economy is always in equilibrium by its very nature, which is not true for a market economy. This fact is not recognized by conventional economic theory.

The conventional theory is based on the model of a general equilibrium, formulated by Léon Walras in the nineteenth century. He constructed a mathematical model of a quasi-market economy based on multilateral barter, in which all exchanges occur at the same moment. There is always perfect information. Once exchange takes place, all prices are equilibrium prices. The amount of resources is understood as given exogenously. The equilibrium promotes the optimal use of these given resources. The model can be described by a mathematical system of equations in which all exchange values or relative prices are, together with the quantities of goods supplied and demanded, explained simultaneously. Time has no importance. Furthermore, there is no need for money as a means of payment because all goods are exchanged directly for each other. In principle, the participants in the market are self-sufficient "households," who produce the majority of goods they need for themselves. They exchange only a small part of goods,

H.C. Binswanger, *The Growth Spiral*, DOI 10.1007/978-3-642-31881-8_13,

which they possess in a greater quantity than needed by themselves, for goods which they do not possess in a sufficient quantity.

The reality of the modern economy differs fundamentally from this model. Today's real-world markets do not resemble Walras' artificial "market" where millions of people would exchange million of goods simultaneously at equilibrium prices. Such a "market" à la Walras can only be a fiction. It was rather the introduction of money which promoted multilateral markets. Money allows buying and selling of any particular good according to supply and demand of this good independent of supply and demand of other goods, potentially at different places and at different times.

Moreover, money made it possible to build artificial economic units, called firms, which need advances of money in order to be able to pay for productive services *before* they earn money by selling their products. These advances of money represent the firm's capital. The deployment of capital is the precondition for transferring production from self-sufficient "households" to firms that can specialize in the production of only a few goods but at large amounts. This led to a tremendous increase in production and productivity on the basis of the division of labor.

The activity of firms was originally limited by the fact that only a small amount of money was available for the formation of capital. This changed with the development of the banking system, which consists of the central bank and commercial banks. In particular, it changed with the possibility of creating money within the banking system, that is, paper money—the banknotes of the central banks—and bank money, that is sight deposits with the banks. The creation of money is effected by banks, which give credits to their customers in form of bank money. Bank money can be converted into paper money. However, paper money, which became a legal tender, can no longer be converted into gold. Due to the fact that the possibility of the conversion of paper money into gold was abandoned, money can, in principle, be produced in an unlimited amount.

However, banks restrict the granting of credits inasmuch as they are only willing to lend new credits to firms if, at the same time, the equity capital of the firm, which bears the main risk, is also raised. In this way, banks are able to keep insolvency risk within reasonable limits. In order to exploit the potential for the granting of credits by the banking system, it was therefore necessary to increase the readiness of firms to obtain equity capital. This was made possible by the creation of joint-stock companies, in which the liability of the shareholders is restricted to the capital invested in the company, that is, to the amount at which the shares had been issued.

Money creation by credits and the formation of stock companies made it also possible to constantly increase the capital invested in the intensification of land use and the exploration and exploitation of raw material and energy, on which the growth of production is based. Since nature does not have to be paid for her service, the increase of production is associated with an increase in the surplus of production over the amount necessary for subsistence of the households. This surplus is divided into wage income (wages exceeding subsistence level), on the one hand, and income that is appropriated by the owners of natural resources and of capital, on the other, according to the prevailing property rights.

The growth process is dominated by a growth imperative. The growth process must continue, once it has started. The reason is as follows: Without a continuous expansion of the amount of money due to the need of financing new investments, which triggers additional demand, the increased supply of products due to the previous period's investments cannot be sold at prices, including profits, which compensate the risk of the investments. If the prices and the profits fall below the minimum level necessary for the compensation of these risks, firms will first reduce new investments but ultimately also replacement investments, entailing an absolute decline of the social product. This leads to a growth imperative in the sense that the alternative to growth is shrinkage and economic crisis.

But, this does not mean that the growth rate has to be as high as possible. A certain critical minimum growth rate is sufficient to compensate the risk of investments and thus to guarantee an amount of investments that is sufficient to avoid fundamental economic crises. Based on plausible assumptions, we have estimated the minimum *global* (!) growth rate around 1.8 %.

Besides the growth imperative, there is, nevertheless, a growth impetus. This growth impetus essentially relates to the organization of firms as joint-stock companies. Shareholders of those companies have a strong incentive to reinvest a part of profits in order to increase their production capacity. This is due to the fact that the price of shares depends crucially on the expected increase of future profits. In turn, future profits depend on an increase in present production capacities. Since, in today's economies, economic activity is dominated by joint-stock companies, the rate of economic growth tends to exceed the critical minimum rate that is necessary for compensating investment risk. In other words, the growth impetus leads to a growth rate that exceeds the rate that is demanded by the growth imperative.

The growth process does not always happen smoothly, however. Growth is threatened by crises, which are the by-product of a growing economy. As these become more frequent, the prospects for growth deteriorate.

Internal barriers to growth primarily result from the discrepancy between the globalization of the economy and the still existing division of money into national currencies. The exchange rates between the individual countries are only in a temporary state of balance. This balance can be endangered by the increase in the level of debt between individual countries and the level of public debt within countries. This danger is aggravated when financial markets are dominated by speculative bubbles and their subsequent collapses. These bubbles are fostered by an increase in the money supply if the money is spent on buying financial assets instead on investments in the production of goods and services. These bubbles, and the subsequent crashes, make the growth process increasingly unstable.

The *external barriers* to growth result from the increasing exploitation of natural resources and the inability of the environment to absorb the ever-increasing amount of waste products and emissions. Certain signs of limits to the supply of resources are already evident today, in particular concerning water and, in part, land and energy. This will result in higher costs of the absorption of emissions and in the increase of prices of natural resources. It may also lead to political conflicts over the distribution of resources.

For the time being, however, the process of economic growth will be able to continue—even it becomes more unstable and more risky—without being restricted by any definitive external barrier, as there is still enough free space into which economic activity may expand. This space consists of all human activities not (yet) incorporated into the monetary process, as well as those areas of nature that have not (yet) been exploited.

However, there is also a growing discrepancy in the opinion about the advantages or disadvantages of economic growth. The *appealing aspects* of economic growth are the advances in medical science and increased longevity, the increase in the comfort of living and working conditions, the "conquering" of the world through increased traveling and access to global information, the transformation of nature into a "playground" in which human activities need no longer be oriented toward subsistence but are instead directed to the enjoyment of life and play, and finally the construction of an additional cyberspace world where, instead of the real world, pictures of it are presented on screens, in exhibition parks, in museums, etc.

These positive aspects of growth are counteracted by the ecological and social risks connected with growth. The *ecological risks* include the risk that nature may be overexploited and "strike back" as a result. The pollution of air, water, and land is increasing despite a wide range of environmental protection activities. The diversity of species is being reduced and the natural landscapes are being depleted. Also, along with new technologies arise new risks that represent a threat to human beings. In this sense, there remain fundamental "limits to growth," as they have been reevaluated by the authors of the first Club-of-Rome Report 30 years after the appearance of the latter.[1] The *social risks* are primarily connected to the increase of population and the concentration of people in rapidly expanding megacities with ten million and more inhabitants. We also have to consider increasing unemployment as a potential risk. On the one hand, this arises from a shrinking of the self-sufficient part of the economy, where people live from their own products. On the other hand, it is due to the continuing substitution of labor through energy. Furthermore, there is an increasing attraction of drugs and crime that is related to the loss of mutual social control due to increasing mobility and an increasing impoverishment of those people who are unable to keep pace with technological progress.

It is an open question whether the gains achieved by the progress of civilization outweigh the ecological and social losses. Different people perceive these gains and losses very differently, according to their personal preferences and their personal situation. These different perceptions must be considered as political factors in the discussion of economic growth.

A preference for the progress of civilization through economic growth has the advantage of being aligned with the growth impetus and the growth imperative. However, should obstacles to growth become stronger, more attention should

[1] See Donella M. Meadows, Jorgen Randers, Dennis L. Meadows (2004).

certainly be paid to the losses associated with growth. As this seems more and more evident, mankind will be forced to seek ways in which the growth spiral could gradually be returned to a cycle. It will then be necessary to develop ideas concerning the design of an economy that is sustainable, that is, that pays attention to the optimal satisfaction of the economic, ecological, and social aspirations of mankind, instead of maximizing growth.

The purpose of this book is to offer an analysis of the modern market economy and its growth dynamics in order to improve the ability to meet future challenges successfully.

Bibliography

Ackermann J (1977) Der Einfluss des Geldes auf das reale Wirtschaftsgeschehen – eine theoretische Analyse. Bern

Allgoewer E (1992) Ökonomische Theoriebildung und Zeit. Diss. St. Gallen

Alvi G (1989) Le seduzioni economiche di Faust. Mailand

Arrow KJ, Debreu G (1954) Existence of an equilibrium for a competitive economy. Econometrica 22:265–290

Arrow KJ, Hahn FH (1971) General competitive analysis. Holden Day, San Francisco

Aspromourgos T (2005) The invention of the concept of social surplus: petty in the Hartlib Circle. Eur J Hist Econ Thought 12(1):1–24

Barro RJ, Sala-i-Martin X (1995) Economic growth. MIT Press, New York

Beltrani G (1999) Monetäre Aspekte der Wirtschaftswachstums, Diss. St. Gallen

Bender A, Kägi W, Mohr E (2002) Informal insurance and sustainable management of common-pool marine resources in Ha'apai, Tonga. Econ Dev Cult Change 50(2):427–440

Bien G (1990) Die aktuelle Bedeutung der ökonomischen Theorie. In: Zievert, Gerd; Held, Klaus; Wieland, Josef (Hrsg) Sozialphilosophische Grundlagen ökonomischen Handelns, Frankfurt a.M

Binswanger HC (1969) Markt und internationale Währungsordnung. Zürich

Binswanger HC (1978) Eigentum und Eigentumspolitik. Zürich

Binswanger HC (1990) Geld und Gleichgewicht. In: Zeitschrift für Wirtschafts- und Sozialwissenschaften, pp 337–358

Binswanger HC (1991a) Geld und Natur: das wirtschaftliche Wachstum im Spannungsfeld zwischen Ökonomie und Ökologie. Stuttgart/Wien

Binswanger HC (1991b) Die Dynamik der Geldwirtschaft, in: ders., Geld und Natur: das wirtschaftliche Wachstum im Spannungsfeld zwischen Ökonomie und Ökologie. Stuttgart/Wien, pp 83–109

Binswanger M (1992) Information und Entropie. Campus-Verlag, Frankfurt, New York

Binswanger M (1999) Stock markets, speculative bubbles and economic growth. Edward Elgar, Cheltenham, Northampton

Binswanger HC (1993) Geld regiert die Welt–John Lockes Geld- und Zinstheorie auf der Grundlage des Merkantilismus. In: Schefold, Bertram (Hrsg) Kommentare zur Faksimile-Ausgabe von John Locke's "some considerations of the consequences of the lowering of interest, and raising the value of money". Düsseldorf, pp 89–127

Binswanger HC (1994) Geld und Wachstumszwang, in: Binswanger, Hans Christoph; Flotow, Paschen von (Hrsg) Geld und Wachstum: zur Philosophie und Praxis des Geldes. Stuttgart/Wien, pp 81–124

Binswanger HC (2000) Wachstum durch Imagination: J.G. Schlossers Theorie der imaginären Bedürfnisse. In: Klump, Rainer (Hrsg) J. Georg Schlosser, Xenocrates, Marburg, pp 147–170

Binswanger HC, von Flotow P (eds) (1994) Geld und Wachstum: zur Philosophie und Praxis des Geldes. Stuttgart/Wien

H.C. Binswanger, *The Growth Spiral*, DOI 10.1007/978-3-642-31881-8,

Blaug M (1999) The formalist revolution or what happened to orthodox economics after World War II? In: Backhouse RE, Creedy J (eds) From classical economics to the theory of the firm. Edward Elgar, Cheltenham, UK, pp 257–280
Bolz N (2002) Das konsumistische Manifest. München
Bortis H (1997) Institution, behaviour and ecomomic theory, Cambridge
Bray F (1957) Voyage from Utopia. London
Bretschger L (1996) Wachstumstheorie. München/Wien
Brosziewski A (1996): Unternehmerisches Handeln in moderner Gesellschaft. Diss. St. Gallen
Brunner K, Meltzer AH (1989) Monetary economics. Blackwell, Oxford
Bücher K (1914) Volkswirtschaftliche Entwicklungsstufen. In: Grundriss der Sozialökonomie; I. Abteilung, Tübingen, pp 1–18
Chipman JS (2005) Contribution of the Older German School to the Development of Utility Theory. In: Christian S (Hrsg) Studien zur Entwicklung der ökonomischen Theorie XX, Berlin, pp 157–259
Clark JB (1931) Distribution of wealth, a theory of wages, interest and profits. MacMillan, New York
Commons JR (1934) Institutional economics, its place in political economy. MacMillan, New York
Commons JR (1956) The economics of collective action. MacMillan, New York
Costanza R et al (1997) An introduction to ecological economies. CRC, Boca Raton, FL
Daly HE (1977) Steady-state economics. W.H. Freeman, San Francisco
Daly HE (2001) Wirtschaftliches Wachstum und Globalisierung in einer vollen Welt. Natur und Kultur 2(2):3–22
de Haes U et al (eds) (2002) Life-cycle impact assessment: striving towards best practice. Setac, Brussels
Debreu G (1959) The theory of value. An axiomatic analysis of economic equilibrium. Yale University Press, New Haven
Dietz R (2000) Simmels "Philosophie des Geldes" als Theorie der Gestalt der Geldwirtschaft. In: Backhaus JG, Stadermann H-J, Georg Simmels Philosophie des Geldes - Einhundert Jahre danach. Marburg, pp 185–208
Domar ED (1946) Capital expansion, rate of growth and employment. Econometrica 14(2):137–147
Domar ED (1957) Essays in the theory of economic growth. Oxford University Press, New York
Dopfer K (2001) Evolutionary economics–framework for analysis. In: ders (ed) Evolutionary economics: program and scope. Kluwer Academic, Boston, pp 1–44
Dopfer K (ed) (2005) Evolutionary economics: a theoretical framework. Cambridge University Press, Cambridge
Dorfner E (1994) Der Zins in der modernen Geldwirtschaft. In: Binswanger HC, Flotow P von (Hrsg) Geld und Wachstum. Stuttgart, pp 134–160
Dosi G, Nelson RR (1994) An introduction to evolutionary theories in economics. Evol Econ 4(3):153–172
Douthwaite R (1999) The ecology of money. Green Books, Foxhole
Dyllick T, Belz F, Schneidewind U (1997) Ökologie und Wettbewerbsfähigkeit. Zürich
Engel E (1857) Die Produktions- und Konsumverhältnisse des Königreichs Sachsen. In: Zeitschrift des Statistischen Büros der Kgl. Sächsischen Ministeriums des Inneren
Faber M (ed) (1986) Studies in Austrian capital theory, investment and time. Springer, New York
Faber M, Manstetten R, Proops J (1996) Ecological economics—concepts and methods. Edward Elgar, Cheltenham
Fisher I (1930) The theory of interest. MacMillan, New York
Forrester JW (1971) World dynamics. Wright-Allen Press, Cambridge, MA
Friedman M (1992) Geld regiert die Welt: neue Provokationen vom Vordenker der modernen Wirtschaftspolitik, Düsseldorf
Gale D (1982) Money: in equilibrium. Cambridge University Press, Cambridge

Gasche UP, Guggenbühl H (2004) Das Geschwätz vom Wachstum. Zürich
Georgescu-Roegen N (1971) The entropy law and the economic process. Cambridge University Press, Cambridge, MA
Gesell S (1991) Die natürliche Wirtschaftsordnung, Gesammelte Werke, Band 11. Lütjenburg
Gray LC (1913) The economic possibilities of conservation. Q J Econ 27(3):497–519
Graziani A (2003) The monetary theory of production. Cambridge University Press, Cambridge
Grossman G, Helpman E (1994) Endogenous innovation in the theory of growth. J Econ Perspect 8(1):23–44
Hagen L (2002) Die monetäre Wahrnehmung der ökonomischen Wirklichkeit—Geld als zentrale Institution der modernen Wirtschaft, Diss. St. Gallen
Hahn LA (1920) Volkswirtschaftliche Theorie des Bankkredits. Tübingen
Hardin G (1968) The tragedy of the commons. Science 162(3859):1243–1248
Harrod RF (1939) An essay in dynamic theory. Econ J 49(193):14–33
Hayek FA (2003) Der Wettbewerb als Entdeckungsverfahren. In: ders., Rechtsordnung und Handelsordnung. Tübingen, pp 132–149
Hein E (2003):Reale and monetäre Analyse: Post-Keynesianismus und Neukeynesianismus im Vergleich. In: Hein E, Heise A, Truger A (Hrsg) Neu-Keynesianismus. Marburg, pp 135–176
Heinsohn G, Steiger O (1996) Eigentum, Zins und Geld. Reinbek
Held M (2005) Nachhaltiges Naturkapital und ökologische Dienstleistungen. In: Beschorner Th, Eger Th (Hrsg) Das Ethische in der Ökonomie–Festschrift für Hans G. Nutzinger. Marburg, pp 503–524
Helmstädter E (1981) Wie bilden sich die Marktpreise nach Adam Smith? In: Neumark F (Hrsg) Studien zur Entwicklung der ökonomischen Theorie I. Berlin, pp 93–109
Herrmann-Pillath C (2001) On the ontological foundations of evolutionary economics. In: Dopfer K (ed) Evolutionary economics: program and scope. Kluwer Academic, Boston, pp 89–139
Hesse G (1986) Liberale Wirtschaftspolitik im evolutorischen Prozess. In: Nutzinger HG (Hrsg) Liberalismus im Kreuzverhör. Frankfurt am Main, pp 79–102
Hildebrand B (1922) Die Nationalökonomie der Gegenwart und Zukunft und andere gesammelte Schriften. Jena
Hirsch F (1995) Social limits to growth. Routledge & Kegan Paul, London
Hodgskins T (1964) Labour defended. Thomas Hodgskins, London
Hoffmann-Kroll R, Schäfer D, Seibel S (1995) Indikatorensystem für den Umweltzustand in Deutschland. Wirtschaft Statistik 8/95:589–597
Holleis W (1985) Das Ungleichgewicht der Gleichgewichtstheorie. Frankfurt a.M.
Jäger A (1999) Leon Walras (1834-1910)–Mathematische Ordnung der als 'entia physica' gedachten Ökonomie. In: ders., Was ist Ökonomie? Marburg
Jöhr WA (1979) Grenzen des Wachstums. In: Siebert H (Hrsg) Umwelt und wirtschaftliche Entwicklung. Darmstadt, pp 279–310
Keynes JM (1936) The general theory of employment, interest and money. MacMillan, London
Keynes JM (1937) The 'Ex-ante' theory of the rate of interest. Econ J 47:663–669
Keynes JM (1971) A treatise on money, The collected writings of J.M.K., vol V/VI. MacMillan, London
Kirchgässner G (1997) Auf der Suche nach dem Gespenst des Ökonomismus. Analyse und Kritik – Zeitschrift für Sozialwissenschaften 19:127–152
Kirchgässner G (2000) Homo oeconomicus, 2.A. Tübingen
Klausinger H (1991) Theorien der Geldwirtschaft—Von Hayek und Keynes zu neueren Ansätzen. Berlin
Klump R (2000) Johann Georg Schlosser (1739–1799): Leben und Werk. In: ders.: J. Georg Schlosser, Xenocrates. Marburg, pp 87–112
Knies K (1883) Die Politische Ökonomie vom Standpunkt der geschichtlichen Methode. Braunschweig
Kraus JX (2000) Die Stoa und ihr Einfluss auf die Nationalökonomie. Marburg
Kümmel R (1980) Growth dynamics of the energy dependent economy. In: Eichhorn W, Henn R (eds) Mathematical systems in economics, vol 54. Oeigeschalger, Gunn & Hain, Cambridge, MA

Kurz HD (1999) From classical rent theory to marginal productivity theory. In: Mongiori G, Petri F (eds) Value, distribution and capital. Taylor and Francis, London, pp 145–164
Kurz H, Salvadori N (1995) Theory of production—a long period analysis. Cambridge University Press, Cambridge
Lange O (1942) Say's law: a restatement and criticism. In: ders., Studies in mathematics and econometrics. Chicago
Lavezzi A (2003) Smith, Marshall and Young on division of labour and economic growth. Eur J Hist Econ Thought 10(1):81–108
Law J (1934) Money and trade considered with a proposal for supplying the nation with money. In: Harsin P (Hrsg) Ouvres Complètes. Paris, tome 1
Lehmann-Waffenschmidt M (ed) (2001) Perspektiven des Wandels—Evolutorische Ökonomie in der Anwendung. Marburg
Lindenberger D, Kümmel R (2002) Thermodynamics and economics. Postantistatic Econ Rev 14
Locke J (1946) The second treatise of civil government. Blackwell, Oxford
Löwe J (1995) Der unersättliche Mensch. Amsterdam
Löwe J (1998) KontextuelleTheorie der Volkswirtschaft–Der Ansatz von Karl Knies als Grundlage künftiger Wirtschaftspolitik
Lucas RE (1972) Expectations and the neutrality of money. J Econ Theory 4(2):103–125
Lucas RE (1973) Some international evidence on output-inflation tradeoffs. Am Econ Rev 63(3):326–335
Lucas RE (1988) On the mechanics of economic development. J Monet Econ 22(1):3–42
MacLeod HC (1889) Lectures on credit and banking. London
Mangoldt Hv (1971) Grundriss der Volkswirtschaftslehre. Stuttgart
Marshall A (1890) Principles of economics, vol 1., London
Marshall A (1923) Money, credit and commerce. London
Marshall A (1961) Principle of Economics, vol 1., Ninth Edition, London
Marx K (1972) Das Kapital, Erstes Buch. Berlin
Marx K, Engels F (1956) Werke. Berlin
Meadows DM, Meadows DL, Randers J, Behrens WW (2004) Limits to growth. Report for the Club of Rome, New York
Meadows DM, Randers J, Meadows DL (1972) Limits to growth—30-year update. White River Junction, VT
Mill JS (1899) Principles of political economy, 2 vols. D. Appleton, New York
Miller MH, Modigliani F (1975) Dividendenpolitik, Wachstum und die Bewertung von Aktiven. In: Hax H, Laux H (Hrsg) Die Finanzierung der Unternehmung. Köln
Minsch J (1988) Ursache und Verursacherprinzip im Umweltbereich – Zur theoretischen Fundierung einer verursacherorientierten Umweltpolitik, Diss. St. Gallen
Minsch J et al (1996) Mut zum ökologischen Umbau. Basel
Mitchell WC (1913) Business cycles. National Bureau of Economic Research, New York
Mitchell WC (1950) The backward art of spending money. Augustus M. Kelly, New York
Modigliani F, Miller MH (1955) The cost of capital, corporation finance, and the theory of investment. Am Econ Rev 55(3):516–525
Möller T (1986) Energie im gesamtwirtschaftlichen Produktionsmodell: Ein Dritter Produktionsfaktor und sein Einfluss auf die langfristige Entwicklung einer energieabhängigen Wirtschaft, Diss. St. Gallen
Nutzinger HG (1974) Die Stellung des Betriebes in der sozialistischen Wirtschaft. Frankfurt
Onken W (1999) Silvio Gesell und die Natürliche Wirtschaftordnung. Lütjenburg
Pasinetti L (2005) The Sraffa-enigma: introduction. Eur J Hist Econmic Thought 12(3):373–378
Patinkin D (1965) Money, interest, prices. Harper & Row, New York
Pearce DW, Turner RK (1990) Economics of natural resources and the environment. Johns Hopkins University Press, Herfordshire
Petty W (1691) Political anatomy of Ireland. D. Brown and W. Rogers, London

Peukert H (2005) Social accountability: Der Weg zu einer menschengerechten Weltordnung. In: Beschorner Th, Eger Th (Hrsg) Das Ethische in der Ökonomie - Festschrift für Hans G. Nutzinger. Marburg, pp 403–430
Pigou AC (1951) Value of money. In: Readings in monetary theory. Blakiston, Philadelphia
Preiser E (1961a) Der Kapitalbegriff und die neuere Theorie. In: ders., Bildung und Verteilung des Volkseinkommens, 2. Auflage. Göttingen, pp 99–123
Preiser E (1961b) Erkenntniswert und Grenzen der Grenzproduktivitätstheorie. In: ders.: Bildung und Verteilung des Volkseinkommens, 2. A. Göttingen, pp 265–289
Priddat BP (2000) Johann Georg Schlosser: Ein deutscher Antiphysiokrat. In: Klump R (Hrsg) J. Georg Schlosser, Xenocrates. Marburg, pp 113–146
Priddat BP (2002)Theoriegeschichte der Wirtschaft. München
Proudhon P-J (1847) Die Widersprüche der Nationalökonomie oder die Philosophie der Not, 2 Bände. Leipzig
Proudhon P-J (1849) Das Recht auf Arbeit, das Eigentumsrecht und die Lösung der sozialen Frage. Leipzig
Quesnay F (1924) Das Naturrecht, Analyse der Wirtschaftstabellen, Allgemeine Grundsätze der wirtschaftlichen Regierung eines ackerbaubetreibenden Reiches. Jena
Racek A (2001) Befreiungsphilosophie des Geldes. Wien, München
Ricardo D (1951) On the principles of political economy and taxation. Cambridge University Press, Cambridge
Richardson GB (1975) Adam Smith on competition and increasing returns. In: Skinner AS, Wilson T (eds) Essays on Adam Smith. Oxford
Rieger W (1926) Einführung in die Privatwirtschaftslehre. Nürnberg
Riese H (2001) Aspekte eines monetären Keynesianismus. In: ders., Grundlegungen eines monetären Keynesianismus, Band 1. Marburg
Rieter H (1994) Historische Schulen. In: Issing O (Hrsg) Geschichte der Nationalökonomie, 3.A. München, pp 127–162
Rieter H (2002) Deutsche Geldtheorie im 19. Jahrhundert—mehr als nur ein Echo englischer Debatten? In: Schefold B (Hrsg) Exogenität und Endogenität. Marburg, pp 13–55
Rogall H (2006) Volkswirtschaftslehre für Sozialwissenschaftler. Wiesbaden
Romer PM (1986) Increasing returns and long run growth. J Polit Econ 94(5):1002–1037
Romer PM (1990) Endogenous technological change. J Polit Econ 98(5):71–102
Romer D (1996) Advanced macroeconomics. McGraw Hill, New York
Rüegg-Stürm J (1996) Controlling für Manager. Zürich
Samuelson PA (1962) Parable and realism in capital theory: the surrogate production function. Rev Econ Stud 29(3):193–206
Samuelson PA (1966) Economists and the history of ideas. In: ders., The collective scientific papers of Paul A. Samuelson, Band 2. Cambridge, MA
Samuelson PM, Nordhaus WD (1995) Economics. McGraw-Hill, New York
Say J-B (1817) Traité d'Economie Politique, 1. Band, 4. Auflage. Paris
Sayers RS (1964) Modern banking, 6. Auflage. Oxford
Schefold B (1971) Theorie der Kuppelproduktion, Diss. Basel
Schefold B (1981a) Nachfrage und Zufuhr in der klassischen Ökonomie. In: Neumark F (Hrsg) Studien zur Entwicklung der ökonomischen Theorie I. Berlin, pp 53–91
Schefold B (1981b) Die Marktpreise bei Adam Smith—eine Erwiderung. In: Neumark F (Hrsg) Studien zur Entwicklung der ökonomischen Theorie I. Berlin, pp 111–115
Schefold B (1999) Use value and the commercial knowledge of commodities. In: Mongiori G, Petri F (eds) Value, distribution and capital. Taylor and Francis, London, pp 122–144
Schlosser JG (1777) Politische Fragmente. Leipzig
Schlosser JG (2000) Xenocrates oder über die Abgaben, Nachdruck. In: Klump R (Hrsg) J. Georg Schlosser, Xenocrates. Marburg
Schmidt K-H (1994) Merkantilismus, Kameralismus, Physiokratie. In: Issing O (Hrsg) Geschichte der Nationalökonomie, 3. Auflage. München, pp 36–62

Schmidt J (1998) Wachstum und Verteilung in der Geldwirtschaft—Das wissenschaftliche Werk Erich Preisers (1900–1967). Marburg
Schumpeter JA (1926) Theorie der Wirtschaftlichen Entwicklung. Leipzig
Schumpeter JA (1980) Kapitalismus, Sozialismus und Demokratie. München
Schwarz G (2000) In: Reflexion, Liberales Institut Zürich (Hrsg.)
Senf B (2005) Giralgeldschöpfung der Geschäftsbanken—Mythos oder Realität? In: ders., Der Tanz um den Gewinn. Lütjenburg, pp 88–110
Shackle GLS (1968) Recent theories concerning the nature and role of interest. In: Survey of economic theory—money, interest and welfare, vol 1. MacMillan, London, pp 108–153
Sieferle RP (2003) Der Europäische Sonderweg: Ursache und Faktoren, 2. Auflage. Stuttgart
Siegel JJ (2000) The shrinking equity premium. J Portfolio Manage 26:10–17
Simmel G (1889) Philosophie des Geldes. Frankfurt a.M
Smith A (1976) An inquiry into the nature and causes of the wealth of nations. Clarendon, Oxford
Solow R (1956) A contribution to the theory of economic growth. Q J Econ 70(1):65–94
Solow R (1957) Technical change and the aggregate production function. Rev Econ Stat 1957:312–320
Solow R (1994) Perspectives on growth theory. J Econ Perspect 8(1):45–54
Spahn H-P (1999) Makroökonomie, 2. Auflage. Berlin
Spiegel HW (1971) The growth of economic thought, 3. Auflage. Durham, NC
Spremann K (1991) Investition und Finanzierung, 4. Auflage. München
Sraffa P (1925) Sulle Relazioni fra Costo e Quantita Prodotta. Annuali di Economia 277–328
Sraffa P (1926) The laws of returns under competitive condition. Econ J 36:535–550
Sraffa P (1960) Production of commodities by means of commodities. Cambridge University Press, Cambridge
Stahlmann V (1994) Umweltbewusstes Management trotz Wachstumszwang. In: Binswanger HC, von Flotow P (Hrsg) Geld und Wachstum. Stuttgart, pp 195–210
Bundesamt für Statistik (2000) Schweizer Landesindex der Konsumentenpreise, Neuchâtel
Steurer R (2004) Politische Manifestationen einer wissenschaftlichen Auseinandersetzung: Die Wachstumskontroverse im Spiegel der deutschen Wirtschafts- und Umweltpolitik. Zeitschrift für Umweltpolitik und Umweltrecht 3:349–390
Stolper W (1994) Geschichte und Theorie in der Analyse des kapitalistischen Prozesses, Walter Adolf Jöhr Vorlesung 1994, Forschungsgemeinschaft für Nationalökonomie an der Universität St. Gallen (Hrsg.), St. Gallen
Straubhaar T (2005) Den Arbeitsmarkt entfesseln. Schweizer Monatshefte, Okt/Nov
Streissler E (1999) Einführung. In: ders. (Hrsg) Adam Smith, Untersuchung über Wesen und Ursachen des Reichtums der Völker, Band 1. Düsseldorf
ten Brink C (1995) Die Begründung der Marktwirtschaft in der Römischen Republik. Bern
Tenne H (1988) Growth. Newbury Park, CA
Tirole J (1997) The theory of industrial organization. Cambridge, MA
Turgot AJR (1981) Betrachtungen über die Bildung und Verteilung der Reichtümer, übersetzt von Marguerite Kuczynski. Berlin
Ulrich P (1997) Integrative Wirtschaftsethik. Bern
Veblen T (1889) The theory of the leisure class. MacMillan, New York
Veblen T (1923) Absentee ownership and business enterprise in recent times, the case of America. New York
von Böhm-Bawerk E (1889) Positive Theorie des Kapitals. Innsbruck
von Flotow P (1994) Geld und Wachstum in der 'Philosophie des Geldes'—die Doppelrolle des Geldes. In: Binswanger HC, von Flotow P (Hrsg) Geld und Wachstum. Stuttgart, pp 32–60
von Wieser F (1914) Theorie der Gesellschaftlichen Wirtschaft. In: Grundriss der Sozialökonomik, 1. Abteilung, Wirtschaft und Wirtschaftswissenschaft. Tübingen
Walras L (1900) Eléments d'économie politique pure, 4. Auflage. Lausanne
Walras L (1936) Etudes d'économie politique appliquée. Lausanne
Weber U (1998) Keynes, Sraffa und die Theorie des ökonomischen Überschusses. Fribourg

Weismahr JA (1992) The factors of production of evolutionary economics. In: Witt U (Hrsg) Explaining process and change. Ann Arbor, pp 67–79
Weissmahr JA (2001) Evolutionary economics for the eco-industrial age. In: Lorenz H-W, Meyer B (Hrsg) Studien zur Evolutorischen Ökonomie IV. Berlin, pp 225–251
Wicksell K (1967) Lectures on political economy, vols 1, 2. Augustus M. Kelley, New York
Wicksteed PH (1894) An essay on the coordination of the laws of distribution, London
Witt U (2001) Evolutionary economics, an interpretative survey. In: Dopfer K (ed) Evolutionary economics: program and scope. Kluwer Academic, Boston, pp 45–88
Witt U (2002) Wirtschaftswachstum—was geschieht auf der Nachfrageseite?, Walter Adolf Jöhr-Vorlesung 2002, Forschungsgemeinschaft für Nationalökonomie an der Universität St. Gallen, Hrsg., St. Gallen
Woll A (1984) Allgemeine Volkswirtschaftslehre, 8. Auflage. München
World Energy Council (1995) Annual report 1995. WEC, London
Young AA (1999) Increasing returns and economic progress. In: Mehrling PG, Sandilands RJ (eds) Money and growth—selected papers of Allwyn Abbott Young. Routledge, London, pp 49–61
Ziegler L (1927) Sinn und Ziel des Wirtschaftens. In: ders., Zwischen Mensch und Wirtschaft. Darmstadt, pp 126–162

MIX
Papier aus verantwortungsvollen Quellen
Paper from responsible sources
FSC® C105338

If you have any concerns about our products,
you can contact us on
ProductSafety@springernature.com

In case Publisher is established outside the EU,
the EU authorized representative is:
Springer Nature Customer Service Center GmbH
Europaplatz 3, 69115 Heidelberg, Germany

Printed by Libri Plureos GmbH
in Hamburg, Germany